Chinese Art and Design

THE
T.T. TSUI
GALLERY OF CHINESE ART

Chinese Art and Design

EDITOR
Rose Kerr

TEXTS
Rose Kerr · Verity Wilson · Craig Clunas

PHOTOGRAPHY
Ian Thomas

DESIGN
Patrick Yapp

VICTORIA AND ALBERT MUSEUM

Published by the Victoria and Albert Museum
First published 1991

© Trustees of the Victoria and Albert Museum

British Library Cataloguing in Publication Data
Kerr, Rose 1953–
    Chinese art and design: the T. T. Tsui Gallery of
    Chinese Art.
    1. Chinese plastic arts, history
    I. Title II. Wilson, Verity 1947– III. Clunas, Craig
    1954– IV. Victoria and Albert Museum
    730.0951

ISBN 1 85177 017 8 paper
ISBN 1 85177 039 9 cloth

Cartography by Lee Gibbons and Rodney Paull
Index by Robert Hood
Typesetting by Southern Positives and Negatives (SPAN),
Lingfield, Surrey
Chinese typesetting by Mitaka
Origination and printing by Arnoldo Mondadori,
Verona, Italy

Front cover:
TABLE FRONTAL
Tapestry woven silk
1600–1700, Ming-Qing dynasties
90 × 87 cm
FE.37-1972
Given by Sir Harry and Lady Garner
明末 — 清初刻絲桌布

Back cover:
JADE PLAQUE FOR SEWING ON TO CLOTHING
1500–1620, Ming dynasty
Diameter 11.2 cm
1643–1882
Wells Bequest
明玉服飾佩

Reverse of cover:
SECTION OF A BOLT OF SILK
Design in gauze weave against a plain weave ground
1900–30, Qing dynasty-Republic
Whole bolt 1496 × 74.5 cm
FE.114-1983
Addis Bequest
清末 — 民國初紗紋錦（部分）

Contents

Prefaces

It has been ten years since my first visit to the Victoria and Albert Museum when I was enormously impressed by the superb quality of its Chinese Collection and the total dedication of its staff. That impression has grown into admiration and I derive much pleasure from visiting and re-visiting the Museum each time I am in London. There is no doubt that this Chinese Collection, which is not only wonderful but vast, should have a permanent home for exhibition. That this should be possible within the Victoria and Albert Museum further emphasises the strong cultural links between Great Britain and China. I am extremely honoured to be associated with this project.

T. T. Tsui

The Victoria and Albert Museum acquired its first Chinese objects in 1852 and has continued from that year to build up its East Asian collections. Today, the Museum houses an incomparable treasury of Chinese bronzes, ceramics, jades, lacquer, furniture, cloisonné enamel, ivory, wood, bamboo, paintings and textiles. In many areas, for example furniture and textiles, the V&A holdings are among the best study resources outside China itself. The Far Eastern Section, founded in 1970, has augmented these collections, paying particular attention to the twentieth century. A vigorous programme of interpretative work has furthered the Section's role as a centre of research for East Asian material culture. It has not, however, been possible before now to do full justice to a display of Chinese art; conservation requirements for delicate paintings and textiles mean that many of these precious items are seen for the first time in our new gallery, the T. T. Tsui Gallery of Chinese Art.

The new gallery has been made possible through the generous support of a Chinese patron, Mr T. T. Tsui. It is his and our wish that the splendour and greatness of Chinese culture should be made accessible to a very wide audience. We believe it is especially important to attract Chinese visitors, both from abroad and from our own Chinese community in Britain, and for this reason all labelling in the gallery is in both English and Chinese. The Museum is deeply grateful for Mr Tsui's interest and support, which have given birth both to the gallery and to this excellent publication.

Armstrong of Ilminster
Chairman of the Board of Trustees of the Victoria and Albert Museum

Introduction

T HE Victoria and Albert Museum was founded after the Great Exhibition of 1851, using some of the profits from that seminal event in London. One aim of the Museum was to promote high standards of excellence among manufacturers and designers and although the collections have grown and developed, it adheres to that purpose. Among the first items to be purchased in 1852 were Chinese pieces such as porcelain and copper decorated in coloured enamels. Many of these early acquisitions were contemporary and it is typical of the period that they were viewed as part of an integrated collection of ornamental art, with no special emphasis laid on their Chinese origins. A contemporary catalogue, quoted in museum records, discussed the pieces in terms of design and form:

> In all the preceding examples direct imitation of nature is avoided, and the suggestions of nature are conventionalized. Careful attention is paid to distribution of quantities; to form . . . and to colour.

In the years between 1852 and 1991 the East Asian collections have been built up through a mixture of judicious purchases and benefactions, so that today the Museum houses a priceless treasury of Chinese art. There have been gifts and bequests both large and small, but all of them important. Space precludes a complete list of donors and their contributions; the few that are included here appear because of their historical congruity.

In the 1860s the artist James Abbott McNeill Whistler (1834–1903) was instrumental in spreading a fashion for Chinese blue and white porcelain, and subsequent public demand for enamelled 'famille verte', 'famille noire' and 'famille rose' porcelain led to the formation of large private collections by connoisseurs. Noteworthy among such collections was that of George Salting, who died in 1909 leaving 1,405 Chinese ceramics to the Museum. The major part of the Salting Collection comprises luxury items exported from China to the West in the seventeenth and eighteenth centuries. As such it has no counterpart in China and continues to amaze and delight Chinese visitors.

From the early twentieth century Westerners working in China were alerted to the scale and scope of Chinese material culture. Their research, based on Chinese scholarship and on the finds unearthed from the ground in the course of railway-building and other projects, revolutionised the collecting of Chinese art in the West. Artefacts dating from the Neolithic period to the eighteenth century were appreciated and studied. Their scope is epitomised in the collection of George Eumorfopoulos, many of whose pre-eminent art objects came to the Museum between 1935 and 1939.

In the post-war years the V&A continued to augment its Chinese holdings in a methodical manner. Many of its finest acquisitions were made in the 1950s, 60s and

70s, guided by the man who became the first Keeper of the Far Eastern Section, John Ayers. The Section, founded in 1970, was responsible for extending the collection in several important areas, among them the peerless assemblage of Chinese furniture. Since 1983 the Department has sustained momentum both through acquisition and research, paying particular attention to the twentieth century.

In 1988 the development of the Chinese Collection was given a fresh boost through Mr T. T. Tsui's generous gift of £1.25 million. The money has not been used to buy new objects, but rather to further the interpretation of our existing treasures through the installation of a new gallery, the evolution of an educational programme and the publication of this book.

The aim of these ventures is to increase public understanding and awareness of the richness of Chinese culture and history. Of course, it would be possible to achieve this in a number of ways. The present approach, resulting from surveys of the opinions of colleagues and of visitors, is to interpret objects through their patterns of use. For this reason and guided by the limits of the V&A's collections, the subject has been framed through six different areas of usage. These are: in burial; in religious worship; in everyday life; for eating and drinking; at court; and in the possession of collectors. It is hoped that this organisation of material will prove accessible to a wide public and in particular that it can be applied to educational syllabuses.

It follows that this book is not a general history of China. Neither were the objects in the collection originally selected to illustrate the six themes outlined above, as they were acquired at many different times for a variety of different reasons. The present choice and interpretation is the work of the authors alone.

In the T. T. Tsui Gallery of Chinese Art all the exhibits are labelled in both English and Chinese. In the book it has only been possible to include plate captions in Chinese, although it is to be hoped that a full Chinese translation may follow some day. In addition to rendering information accessible to Chinese visitors, the use of two languages provides interesting comparisons in methodology, particularly in the field of dating. In English, although historical periods may be mentioned, a date in years is also provided. In Chinese, it is traditional to date objects to a historical dynasty and sometimes to a reign period within that dynasty. This practice is uniquely Chinese, for though dynasties conform in a broad sense to comparable English ruling houses ('the Tudors', 'the Stuarts') their attribution is at once more universal and more specific.

A Chinese dynasty was formed when one group among many contending factions, headed by a forceful individual, managed to seize overall military control of significant areas of the Chinese heartland. This victorious group was quick to consolidate its power base through a variety of military and bureaucratic means, but the most immediate and important thing was the selection of a name by which the ruling house would be known. The choice of a name was significant and some names of dynasties had suitable connotations; for example, the 'ming' of Ming dynasty means bright or brilliant, while the 'qing' of Qing dynasty means clear or pure. The various rulers who succeeded one another within each dynasty also had individual names, which were not their personal family names but special titles assumed when they ascended the throne. Thus the name of the Xuande emperor of the Ming dynasty means 'Demonstrable Virtue' while that of the Qianlong emperor of the Qing dynasty means 'Heaven's Majesty'.

In the Chinese view the power of an emperor to rule was conferred on him by the Mandate of Heaven, and the rise and fall of dynasties was controlled by a cycle that linked military and political power with the waxing and waning of moral virtue in the ruling house. This progression through combat, victory and consolidation to eventual overthrow was linked with a parallel sequence of idealism, dogmatism, corruption and oppression, and is a pattern still observed in twentieth-century China by some analysts. While the material in this book is not interpreted through traditional dynastic chronology, the artefacts illustrated here come from every period of Chinese history, from the Stone Age to the present day.

As far as dating conventions are concerned, a complete list of the Chinese dynasties with their dates is provided in the chronology on page 19. In picture captions a greater precision has been attempted, so that where possible a period of years within the dynasty has been included. Some Chinese art objects are marked with the name of the emperor who was on the throne at the time of their manufacture. In this case, the emperor's reign period with dates is included. In the case of an apocryphal mark, the actual date of manufacture is also provided.

The book has been designed to a common format with that of the books accompanying the Toshiba Gallery of Japanese Art and Design, and the Chinese Export Art and Design Gallery. This format does not permit footnotes, but some of the wide variety of sources drawn on by the authors are mentioned here.

Suning Sun-Bailey translated the picture captions, gave general editorial advice and suggested formats. Her assistance has been invaluable.

Nigel Wood's work on clay bodies and glazes was consulted for the first section of the book. The chapter on burial was built on research foundations laid down by James L. Watson, Evelyn S. Rawski and Susan Naquin. Jessica Rawson's advice was sought on the dating and decoration of bronzes, James Watt on the dating of jades and Sarah Allan for ideas on Shang philosophy. The research conducted by John Larson, Anne Brodrick and Richard Cook in the course of conservation contributed valuable information to the chapters on both burial and worship. Jean M. James is acknowledged for her work on the Wu family shrines and Han funerary art, and Ellen Johnston Laing for her study of Jin material culture. Helen B. Chapin has written about the iconography of Buddhist images in Yunnan. Both W. Zwalf and John Guy provided information on Buddhist history and the former also gave help on the Khotanese inscription on one of the Tang banners. The chapter on living includes views based on Derek Gillman's work on ivory carving, information from Frances Wood on Chinese domestic architecture and ideas from Wang Yarong and Wang Xu about textile furnishings. The pioneering work of a group of scholars led by K. C. Chang influenced the chapter on eating and drinking, while research presented at the 1977 International Symposium on Chinese Ceramics at Seattle by Chang Lin-sheng has been incorporated into the paragraphs about the tea-tasting ceremony. Also valuable in the writing of this section was material from the 1984 catalogues of the K. S. Lo Collection in the Flagstaff House Museum of Tea Ware and Jessica Rawson's work on Chinese silver. Margaret Medley's studies of ritual vessels were used in the chapter on ruling, as was Howard Hansford's translation of the poem on the 'Turkish' jade, Thomas Lawton's translation of the title *Xiqing gu jian* and Yang Boda's periodisation of jade carving. Joseph Alsop's ideas on collecting were useful, as was James Watt's identification of the origins of the apocryphal 'Li Zhaodao' painting. The remarks on the philosophical roots of the Oriental Ceramic Society originated from an essay by Rachel Gotlieb.

In the process of bringing the new gallery project to fruition, I should like to cite the initial help and encouragement of Grace Wu Bruce.

The range of skills necesssary to install a major new gallery and to produce a book involve most sections of the Museum. In addition to the authors, the entire staff of the Far Eastern Collection has played a critical role in achieving this goal. Particular mention must be made of Amanda Ward, who has acted with consummate patience and skill as Project Co-ordinator, in addition to rationalising the conservation programme. Anna Jackson planned and executed a complicated photographic programme and Ian Thomas took the superb photographs. Helen White, Louise Hofman, Liz Wilkinson, Ruth Bottomley, Rupert Faulkner and Julia Hutt have assisted willingly with the unglamorous but necessary work which the gallery and book have demanded.

The gallery has provided a signal opportunity to conserve and investigate objects in all media and the staff of every conservation section must be thanked for their hard work, assistance and advice.

Gordon Charlesworth, Stephen King and staff from the Department of Buildings and Estate have administered practical details of design and construction during the project, while Charles Kennett, Nick Johnstone and their teams have arranged its detailed execution.

The innovative flair and attention to detail of Martyn Best (architect), John Csaky, Angela Simpson, Jane Lawrence and their colleagues from Fitch Benoy have resulted in a gallery design which is not only visually exciting, but also one that successfully interprets the V&A's presentational ideas while setting the highest professional standards of museum installation. Tymn Lintell and Piers Lea created the imaginative video programmes in the gallery, with support from Jim Divers.

I have left the most important vote of thanks until last. The main instigator of this project was T. T. Tsui who, together with his wife Amy, has provided constant support, inspiration and encouragement. To him I can only say 謹致薄禮, 略表謝忱 'please accept this small gift with our heartfelt thanks'.

Rose Kerr
Far Eastern Collection
June 1990

Note on Spelling and Pronunciation

The *pinyin* system of romanizing the Chinese script is used throughout, with the exception of certain well established place names such as Peking, Taipei, Canton, Hong Kong and the Yangtze river. This system represents the sounds of Modern Standard Chinese (*putonghua*).

The following few hints may help the reader unfamiliar with the system at least to pronounce words to themselves:

Initial *c–*, as English *ts–*
Initial *q–*, as English *ch–*
Initial *x–*, as English *s–*
Initial *zh–*, as English *j–*

Map of China

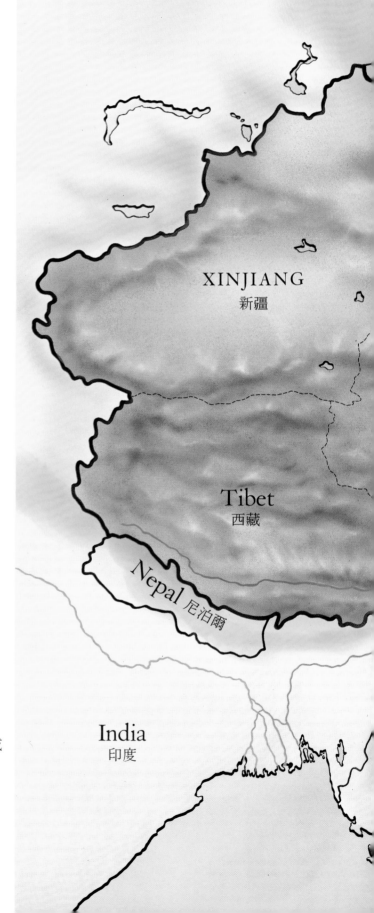

NEIGHBOURING REGIONS

Burma	緬甸
India	印度
Japan	日本
Mongolia	蒙古
Nepal	尼泊爾
North Korea	北朝鮮
South Korea	南朝鮮
Tibet	西藏

PROVINCES

Fujian	福建
Gansu	甘肅
Guangdong	廣東
Hebei	河北
Henan	河南
Hunan	湖南
Inner Mongolia	內蒙古
Jiangsu	江蘇
Jiangxi	江西
Shaanxi	陝西
Shandong	山東
Shanxi	山西
Sichuan	四川
Taiwan	台灣
Xinjiang	新疆
Yunnan	雲南
Zhejiang	浙江

CITIES AND TOWNS

Anyang	安陽
Canton	廣州
Changsha	長沙
Cizhou	磁州
Dehua	德化
Dunhuang	敦煌
Hangzhou	杭州
Hong Kong	香港
Jingdezhen	景德鎮
Kaifeng	開封
Longquan	龍泉
Nanjing	南京
Peking	北京
Shanghai	上海
Suzhou	蘇州
Taipei	台北
Xi'an	西安
Yangzhou	揚州
Yixing	宜興
Zhangzhou	漳州
Zibo	淄博

GEOGRAPHICAL FEATURES

Great Wall	萬里長城
Wutaishan	五台山
Yangtze River	長江
Yellow River	黃河

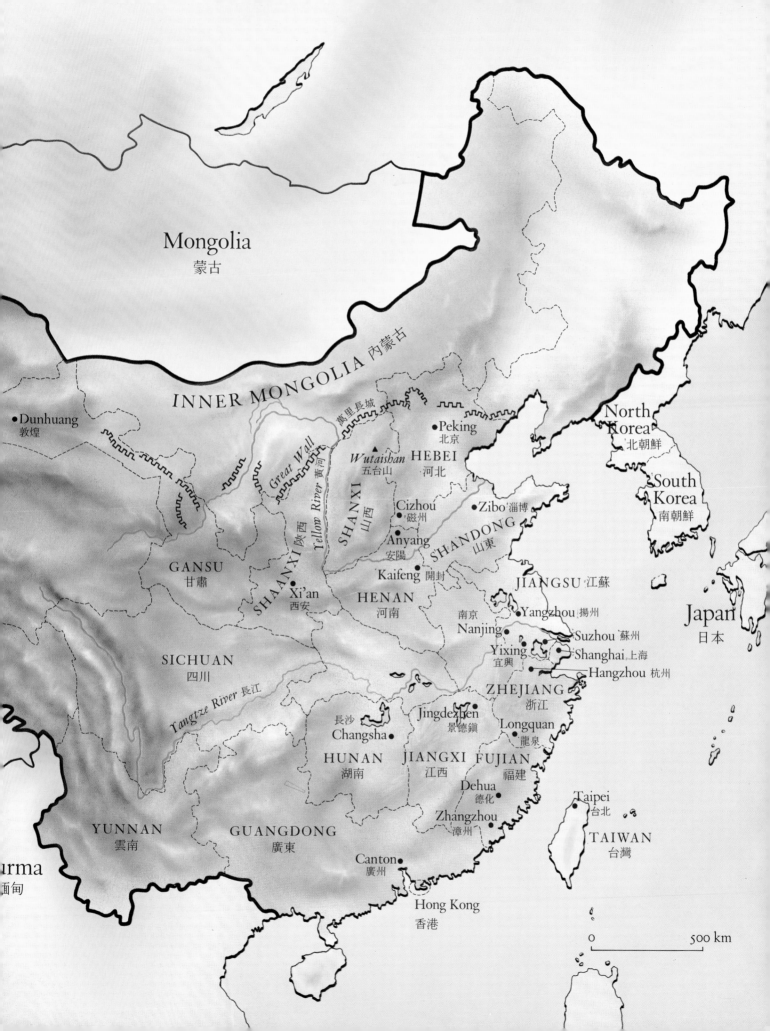

Mongolia
蒙古

INNER MONGOLIA 內蒙古

• Dunhuang
敦煌

Great Wall

萬里長城

Wutaishan
五台山

• Peking
北京

HEBEI
河北

Cizhou
磁州

• Zibo 淄博

SHANXI
山西

Anyang
安陽

SHANDONG 山東

GANSU
甘肅

Yellow River 黃河

Kaifeng 開封

SHAANXI 陝西

Xi'an
西安

HENAN
河南

JIANGSU 江蘇

南京

Yangzhou 揚州

Nanjing

Suzhou 蘇州

SICHUAN
四川

Yixing
宜興

Shanghai 上海

Hangzhou 杭州

Yangtze River 長江

ZHEJIANG
浙江

長沙

Jingdezhen
景德鎮

Longquan
• 龍泉

Changsha •

HUNAN
湖南

JIANGXI
江西

FUJIAN
福建

Dehua
德化

Taipei
台北

Zhangzhou
漳州

TAIWAN
台灣

YUNNAN
雲南

GUANGDONG
廣東

Canton •
廣州

urma
面甸

Hong Kong
香港

North
Korea
北朝鮮

South
Korea
南朝鮮

Japan
日本

0   500 km

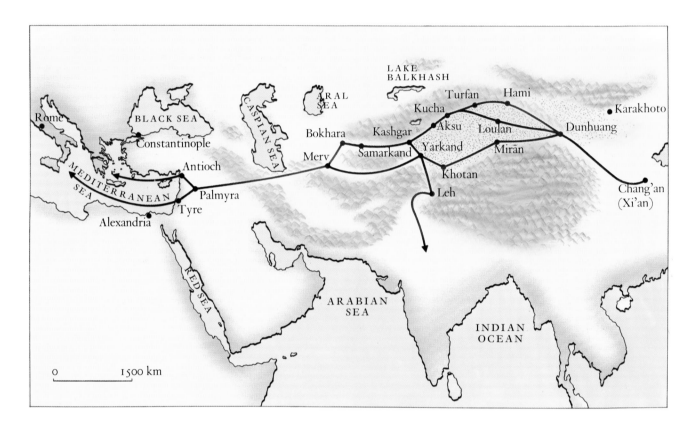

The Silk Routes ＜ 絲綢之路 ＞
linking China and the West

Chronology

Neolithic	新石器時代	about 5000–about 1700 BC
Bronze Age	青銅時代	about 1700 BC–AD 220
(Xia dynasty	夏	historical identity unproven)
Shang dynasty	商	about 1700–1050 BC
Zhou dynasty	周	1050–221 BC
Qin dynasty	秦	221–207 BC
Han dynasty	漢	206 BC–AD 220
Western Han dynasty	西漢	206 BC–AD 8
Eastern Han dynasty	東漢	AD 25–220
Six dynasties period	三國，晋，南北朝	220–580
Sui dynasty	隋	581–618
Tang dynasty	唐	618–906
Liao dynasty	遼	907–1125
Five dynasties	五代十國	907–960
Song dynasty	宋	960–1279
Northern Song dynasty	北宋	960–1127
Southern Song dynasty	南宋	1128–1279
Jin dynasty	金	1115–1234
Yuan dynasty	元	1279–1368
Ming dynasty	明	1368–1644
Qing dynasty	清	1644–1911
Republic	民國	1912–1949
People's Republic	人民共和國	1949–

Four Questions Answered

IN this book as in the gallery, the cultural history of China has been interpreted through six selected themes. The six themes represent only a few of many possible approaches. They are chosen both because they are of general interest, and because they provide excellent reference points for art objects in the collection at the Victoria and Albert Museum.

The six main themes of the book are:

> Burial
> Temple and Worship
> Living (in a rich household)
> Eating and Drinking
> Ruling (the imperial household)
> Collecting.

Before moving on, however, to the main chapters of the book concerned with these themes, four smaller topics connected with the history and understanding of Chinese art will be examined. They are, in fact, some of the topics about which museum visitors most frequently ask questions.

These four smaller topics are dealt with here in the form of questions and answers accompanied by appropriate and relevant objects. It is hoped that this simple approach will serve as an effective and useful introduction to the more complex main themes.

What are these Chinese art objects made of?

Out of a wide range of materials used by craftsmen, five of the most distinctively Chinese have been chosen for illustration (*1*).

Porcelain, made from crushed rock and clay, was first made in China in about AD 600. As the English word 'china' suggests, the material was invented in China; it was made there for more than a thousand years before European kilns discovered the principles of its manufacture. The early fifteenth-century dish on the left of the picture was made at a city called Jingdezhen in south China, where the right rock and clay are found. Porcelain is fired in a very hot kiln at a temperature of more than 1,200° Celsius and its surface is easy to paint and glaze.

Lacquer is the sap of a tree (*rhus verniciflua*), and has been tapped in China since about 3000 BC. Filtered and purified lacquer is applied to a base, usually of wood, and coloured. The red colour of the early fifteenth-century box shown here was achieved by using cinnabar (mercuric sulphide) as a colouring agent. Lacquer is decorated in several ways; by inlaying, painting and incising. This box was decorated by building up many layers of lacquer and then carving them.

Cloisonné enamel takes its name from the barriers of wire (cloisons) which separate enamel colours. The wires are fixed to a metal base, usually copper, glass-

1
PORCELAIN DISH (*back left*)
Xuande reign period mark (1426–35),
Ming dynasty
Diameter 28 cm
1633-1876
明宣德瓷盤

LACQUER BOX (*centre left*)
Yongle reign period mark (1403–24),
Ming dynasty
Diameter 22.2 cm
FE.22-1974
明永樂雕漆盒

CLOISONNÉ CENSER
(*centre right*)
1400–30, Ming dynasty
Height 24 cm
507-1875
明早期招絲琺瑯爐

WOVEN SILK RANK BADGE
(*back right*)
1500–1600, Ming dynasty
35 × 32 cm
FE.11-1986
明中 — 晚期錦識章

JADE CUP (*front*)
1500–1600, Ming dynasty
Width 15 cm
C.1127-1917
明中 — 晚期玉杯

like enamels are applied and the piece is fired in a kiln. The incense burner to the right of the illustration was made in the early fifteenth century, when the technique was newly fashionable in China.

Silk threads are obtained from certain caterpillars called silkworms. The silkworm pushes out silk strands from its lower lip to form a cocoon, which is then unravelled by silkworkers into long filaments. The filaments are strengthened and coloured for use in weaving, embroidery and sewing. The design on the sixteenth-century rank badge was woven from coloured weft (horizontal) threads which completely cover the undyed warp (vertical) threads.

Jade is the name used to embrace a variety of coloured stones, the most valuable of which are the silicates called nephrite and jadeite. Jadeite came from Burma. The main source of Chinese nephrite was the north-western province of Xinjiang, where jade was found as boulders in river beds, and was also mined. Jade is too hard to carve, so abrasive sands are used with grinding and cutting tools to wear away the stone. Chinese jades come in many colours, the most common of which are green and white. The sixteenth-century cup shown at the front is made from nephrite jade.

Where were these art objects made and who made them?

The objects shown (*2*) were made in different types of places. Some were individually created, while others were mass-produced.

The late fifteenth-century porcelain bowl on the left was mass-produced at a large factory in Jingdezhen in south China. Some porcelain factories employed hundreds of people, working on production lines. This bowl passed through the hands of dozens of people when it was being shaped, painted, glazed and fired.

The seventeenth-century white porcelain cup in the foreground was made at a small factory in the town of Dehua in south-east China. The factory may have been family-run, and probably employed only a few people.

The big brown peach on a stand is actually a gourd, grown on a vine inside a peach-shaped mould. It was created by a rich gentleman, as a hobby. On the top is a mark reading 'beautiful object made for enjoyment in the Qianlong era (1736–95)'.

The red lacquer cup and lid on the right were made by top craftsmen employed at the imperial court in Peking. They were made for the Qianlong emperor's court at a time when imperial power and wealth were very great.

The carved bamboo box at the front of the picture is shaped like a section of pine tree and is signed with the name of its maker. He was called Deng Fujia, and he was a master-craftsman who made luxury objects for rich patrons during the reign of the Qianlong emperor.

What is the decoration about?

Many of the patterns and scenes on Chinese art objects come from stories, or carry overt or hidden meanings. Such decorations would be immediately interpreted and understood by most Chinese people, but their meanings are less obvious to people who are not Chinese. It is not the purpose of this book to catalogue designs and their meanings, but five of the many stories and motifs on Chinese objects are shown here as examples (*3*).

2

PORCELAIN BOWL (*left*)
1475–1500, Ming dynasty
Diameter 15.2 cm
C.660-1921
Eccles Gift
明中期瓷碗

PORCELAIN CUP (*centre right*)
1600–1700, Ming-Qing dynasties
Height 7.8 cm
FE.21C-1970
MacNaghten Bequest
明末 — 清初瓷杯

GOURD (*back*)
Qianlong reign period mark
(1736–95), Qing dynasty
Height 22.8 cm
FE.159-1975
Addis Gift
清乾隆葫蘆桃

LACQUER CUP (*back right*)
Qianlong reign period mark
(1736–95), Qing dynasty
Diameter 11.2 cm
FE.66-1974
Garner Gift
清乾隆漆蓋碗

BAMBOO BOX (*front*)
Qianlong reign period (1736–95),
Qing dynasty
Length 11.5 cm
W.338-1910
清乾隆雕竹盒

· The Eight Immortals ·

The Eight Immortals are figures of good luck, linked with wishes for wealth, happiness and a long life. On the early eighteenth-century lantern on the left of the picture they are seen crossing the ocean from their home in the Daoist paradise. These figures from the Daoist religion began to appear on objects in the fourteenth century. Soon they became one of the most common subjects in all Chinese art.

· The West Chamber ·

The West Chamber is China's great love story, and has its origins in a prose tale written during the Tang dynasty (618–906). It tells of the adventures of the talented hero Zhang Junrui and the beautiful girl Cui Yingying. Many obstacles are put in the way of their love before the 'hopeful' ending of the tale. On the tall blue-and-white vase at the back of the picture, which was made in about 1700, the whole story is told from top to bottom like a strip cartoon.

· The Five Sons of Yanshan ·

Dou Yanshan,
Had the right plan.
Taught his five sons.
Each became a great man.

This rhyme comes from a simple history of China once used to teach children to read, the *Three Character Classic*. On the brightly-coloured sixteenth-century Ming dynasty wine jar in the foreground is the elderly Dou Yanshan. His servant points to the direction from which the five sons, wearing splendid official robes, come to pay respects to their father. The five sons and their servants are painted on the back of the jar.

· Dragons ·

In China the dragon is a supernatural being, and one of the twelve animals of the zodiac. Dragons are often linked with the emperors of China and are shown on many items made for them, like the oval vase at the back right of this picture. This magnificent early fifteenth-century piece was probably made for the imperial court. However, many dragon legends connected with fertility and rain were known by ordinary people and an object with a dragon on it may refer to one of these stories instead.

· Bats and Peaches ·

The Chinese word for 'bat' and the word for 'happiness' are both pronounced *fu*. Peaches are the fruit of long life. On the early eighteenth-century dish at the right of the picture, five bats are shown flying out to sea beneath a peach tree growing out of a craggy mountain cliff. This is one of many Chinese patterns that carry a hidden meaning based on a play on words, in this case the traditional birthday greeting 'may your happiness be as deep as the Eastern Sea and may you live to be as old as the Southern Mountain'.

3 (left to right)

PORCELAIN LANTERN
1720–25, Qing dynasty
Height 20.5 cm
C.1270–1910
Salting Bequest
清早期瓷燈

PORCELAIN VASE
About 1700, Qing dynasty
Height 77.5 cm
C.859–1910
Salting Bequest
清早期瓷瓶

PORCELAIN JAR
About 1550, Ming dynasty
Height 24.7 cm
C.67-1954
Forrest Gift
明中期瓷罐

PORCELAIN VASE
Yongle reign period (1403–24),
Ming dynasty
Height 44.8 cm
FE.4-1974
明永樂瓷瓶

PORCELAIN DISH
Yongzheng reign period mark
(1723–35), Qing dynasty
Diameter 16.8 cm
FE.15-1970
MacNaghten Bequest
清雍正瓷碟

How did these Chinese art objects come to be here?

There is a tendency to imagine that objects arrive in museum cases by some mysterious but universal selection process. The truth is that art objects come into museums by different routes. Described here are just five of many ways in which public institutions build up their collections. (*4*)

The eighteenth-century cloisonné enamel incense burner on the left belonged to General Charles Gordon (1833–85), who acquired two famous nicknames through his military exploits: 'Chinese Gordon' and 'Gordon of Khartoum'. The incense burner is probably part of the booty he acquired when British and French troops looted the Summer Palace of the Chinese emperors in 1862. The Museum bought the piece from the auction sale of General Gordon's estate.

The blue cloisonné enamel vase with its wooden stand was purchased in 1984 as part of the Museum's programme to acquire contemporary works. A member of staff went to Peking, a traditional centre of cloisonné enamel production, and bought this vase from a factory there. It was new at the time.

The seventeenth-century copper incense burner at the front of the picture has the signature of a famous maker, Hu Wenming. It passed from collector to collector in China, before being sold in this century to the V&A.

The late Song or Yuan dynasty bronze vase in the centre right was used for flowers in a temple or home. It was later taken to Japan for use in the tea ceremony, or for flower arranging. In 1875 a Paris dealer bought the vase in Japan. The Museum bought it from him the next year, thinking it was Japanese.

The bronze jar for wine on the extreme right of the illustration was buried soon after it was made in about 1000 BC. It has turned green through lying for thousands of years in the earth. It was probably dug up early this century, and left China to enter the international art market. The bronze was bequeathed to the V&A by a collector.

4 (left to right)

CLOISONNÉ CENSER
Qianlong reign period (1736–95),
Qing dynasty
Height 26.4 cm
13-1894
清乾隆招絲琺瑯鼎爐

CLOISONNÉ VASE
1984
Height with stand 42 cm
FE.40-1984
現代招絲琺瑯瓶

COPPER CENSER (*front*)
1600–44, Ming dynasty
Diameter 9.5 cm
M.2699-1931
明晚期紅銅爐

BRONZE VASE
1100–1350, Song-Yuan dynasties
Height 17.5 cm
120-1876
宋 — 元銅瓶

BRONZE JAR, *You*
1050–1000 BC, Zhou dynasty
Height 26 cm
M.186-1935
西周早期銅卣

Tomb chamber from Baisha, Henan
province, dated 1099

Burial in China

THROUGHOUT history and across the world, grave goods have fascinated people and have been avidly collected as treasures. They were made in a wide range of materials and styles, and were often of the finest craftsmanship. They also provide a wealth of information on both material and spiritual cultures, and Chinese grave goods are no exception.

This chapter will look at Chinese funerary items preserved in the collections of the Victoria and Albert Museum. Some of these items were used specifically for burials, while others were the sort of goods used in everyday life and then put into tombs. They cover a wide time span from the Neolithic period (about 5000–1700 BC) to the end of the Ming dynasty (AD 1644), and geographically come from all over China. Most of the pieces shown here came from the burials of rich and socially successful people; there exist very few artefacts to record the deaths of the mass of the poor.

The custom of ritually disposing of the dead, including their burial in tombs, started at the very dawn of Chinese civilisation. Archaeological finds of the Stone Age or Neolithic period inform us that as early as about 5000 BC semi-settled communities had established themselves. These peoples practised rudimentary agriculture and animal husbandry, and established separate burial grounds where they buried their dead. Although there are no written records from these early times, the way in which cemeteries were laid out and the grave goods which are found in them tell us two things. One is that Neolithic peoples believed in an afterlife, and the other that social hierarchies operated, with important people having much grander tombs than others. For example, people of the Hongshan culture in north-east China buried their dead in groups of graves. Large and important tombs occurred amidst many smaller ones. Factors already present in the culture of Stone Age China continued to be important, and are reflected in social organisation right down to the present century.

During the Neolithic period China's vast terrain was inhabited by peoples whose customs varied. Some constructed tombs in the form of round cave chambers, or square pits containing wooden coffins, others built stone chambers with stone cists inside and rocks piled up on the surface to form a simple burial mound. On the basis of different practices and surviving artefacts, archaeologists have given names to these different 'cultures'. This chapter mentions the Yangshao culture of central and north-western China, and the Hongshan and Liangzhu cultures of the north-east and east. It should be remembered, however, that these are contemporary terms and probably have little connection with how Neolithic peoples regarded themselves and their neighbours.

Along the valley of the Yellow River, one of the centres of early Chinese civilisation, village settlements were established. One such village, belonging to what archaeologists call the Yangshao culture, has been excavated at Banpo, near the present-day city of Xi'an. A complete plan of the town's beaten earth foundations is preserved, and many artefacts including pottery have been discovered. The different locations of the dwelling areas, the cemetery, the sites of the meeting house or main hall and of the ceramic kilns, were clearly observed. Large jars were used as storage vessels, and the remains of grains and other foodstuffs have been found inside them. The best large pots were used in burials, and children's bones are sometimes contained within them.

The large jar (5) actually comes from Gansu province in the far north-west of China, an offshoot of the Yangshao culture. It is made of red earthenware coiled in carefully prepared strips and then beaten smooth with a paddle. It was fired in a relatively sophisticated kiln in which the fire was separated from the chamber where the pots were placed, and situated underneath them. An updraft system

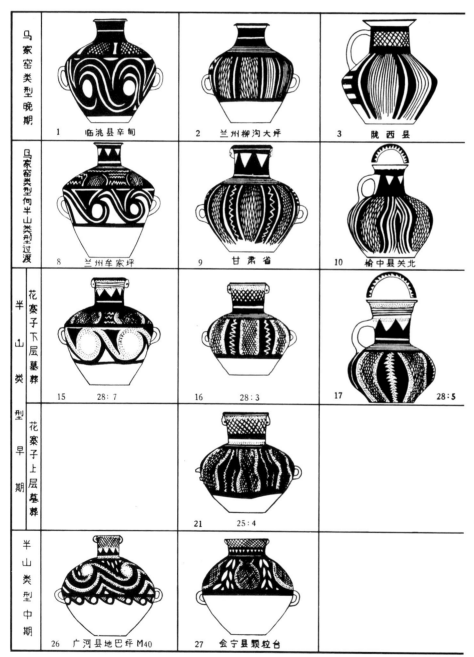

Earthenware jars of the Neolithic Banshan culture, from Gansu province (*left*)
After *Kaogu xuebao* 1980.3

5
BURIAL JAR (*right*)
Earthenware painted with colours
About 2000–1700 BC, Neolithic
Height 38.8 cm
C.286-1938
新石器時代彩陶罐

6 (*overleaf*)
JADE CYLINDERS, *Cong*
About 2800–1900 BC, Neolithic
Heights 15, 27, 40.3, 43.2, 20.4 cm
A.53, 51, 40, 46, 50-1936
新石器時代玉琮

carried the heat of the fire up a channel to bake the pots without damaging them. Temperatures of up to 1,020° Celsius were already being achieved at this early time. After firing, the pot was burnished and painted with intricate and graceful designs, using red and black earth pigments. The meaning of the painted patterns on Stone Age pots is unknown. It is likely, however, that the patterns did have some significance and were not simply decorative.

Chinese Neolithic tombs contained one or more bodies. Single burials were the most common, but couples were buried together, sometimes with their children. This presumably happened when plague or some other calamity struck. Grave goods were placed around and on top of the bodies. Especially common and significant were items made of jade, and recent archaeological discoveries have revealed new and exciting finds from what is called the Liangzhu culture in Zhejiang province. Several distinct jade forms occurred, two of the most important of which were round discs with a hole through the middle, called in Chinese *bi*, and long cylinders called *cong*. Both were ritual objects, but whereas the excavators have concluded that *bi* were sometimes personal possessions, *cong* seem to have had special associations with the shamans or religious leaders of the communities. The ritual importance of jade objects was also a feature of later Chinese culture, particularly during the Han dynasty (206 BC–AD 220).

Some Liangzhu culture *cong* in the Museum's collection are shown here (6). *Cong* are hollow cylinders slightly tapering to one end, with a round inner section and a squared outer section. They stand upright with the broader end at the top. The flat outer sections of *cong* are carved with patterns of lines and circles that form simplified animal or human masks. You can see these masks best if you look at the projecting corners of a *cong* face on. Mask patterns on bronzes (see below) developed from these designs on Neolithic jades.

During the Bronze Age periods of Shang and Zhou (about 1700–221 BC) burial practices developed in size and scale. The tombs of the rulers of the Shang dynasty (about 1700–1050 BC) were enormous. One royal tomb at the burial site at Anyang in Henan province measured 19 by 14 metres, and it has been calculated that it took 7,000 working days to excavate and build. Inside was a wooden burial chamber and thousands of burial goods made of stone, bone, jade, shell, antler, tooth, bronze and pottery. In addition, the Shang rulers took their servants with them into the afterlife. Human and animal sacrifices were frequent; big tombs contained more than 350 bodies. As time went on metal, clay or wooden figures were substituted, until by the Han dynasty human sacrifice had ceased.

Elaborate burials were not merely for the sake of display. Bronze Age rulers believed that the fortunes of the state and those living in it depended on help from the dead spirits of earlier rulers. Good burials showed gratitude, and established the reputation of the king who had just died in the afterworld. It has been suggested that ritual sacrifices accompanying burial were performed to control the natural violence of the universe, by providing surrogate victims in a regular manner. The tombs of princes and rich people echoed royal burials on a smaller scale, and thus were filled with rich grave goods. Many materials were used, the most important being bronze and jade.

As well as vessels for food, Bronze Age tombs also contained items for alcohol, so that the dead could continue to offer sacrifices to the gods and ancestors after death. Illustrated here (7) is a wine container called *zun*, shaped like an owl whose

7
BRONZE VESSEL, *Zun*
1200–1100 BC, Shang dynasty
Height 21 cm
M.5-1935
商晚期銅尊

removable head acts as a lid. *Zun* were used as storage vessels, and were first assigned this name by scholars during the Song period (960–1279). *Zun* come in a wide variety of shapes, including animal and bird forms. The owl's symbolic significance in ancient times remains unknown. In later times its cry was said to resemble a spirit voice, and the bird was said to call away the soul.

The bronze vessel (8) is called *li* in Chinese. The *li* stands on three legs and has a three-lobed body. This shape first occurred in pottery during the Neolithic period,

Bronze vessels of the Shang dynasty
After *Kaogu xuebao* 1979.2 *(left)*

8 (right)
BRONZE VESSEL, *Li*
1400–1200 BC, Shang dynasty
Height 26 cm
M.3-1935
商中 — 晚期銅鬲

when the lobed body and legs were hollow right down their length. Thus they presented the largest possible surface to the flames. In the Bronze Age *li* were used as cauldrons for cereals, and had handles on the rim. The vessel illustrated is simple in both form and surface design. More sophisticated bronzes have complex mask patterns on their bodies, known in Chinese as *taotie*. The mask pattern on this *li* is made up of spiral shapes and a protruberant eye, which come together on both sides of raised flanges. The reason that this *li* is so simple is that it dates to a relatively early phase of the Bronze Age, and was probably made in Shaanxi province, away from metropolitan centres.

Many jades were found inside Bronze Age tombs, including pieces like those shown here (*9*). The two jade blades in the middle and at the bottom of the picture are honed to a fine cutting edge. They would not have been strong enough to use as real weapons, and it is likely that they were merely ceremonial. The weapon at the top, called in Chinese *ge*, has a jade blade fitted into a bronze handle. The handle is in the shape of a dragon's head with long curled snout and beneath it is a foot with claws.

During the Han dynasty burial practices changed again. From excavated tombs and literary texts we know something about the beliefs of the time. When a person died his inner spirit or soul became detached from his body. People were believed to have two souls. The first was called *hun*, and was regarded as an emanation of the *yang* side of the personality (see p.60). After death this soul ascended to paradise where it fitted into the heavenly hierarchy at the same level as the deceased had attained in earthly society. The second more material soul was called *po*, and it came from the *yin* side of the personality. After death this spirit returned to earth as a *gui* spirit, and took up residence in the tomb. Evil spirits that haunted the world were usually *hun* or *gui*. The Chinese believed very strongly in the visitation of both good and evil spirits, and this was another reason why death and burial needed to be observed in correct ways. When the body and soul were first separated, the dead person was believed to feel some degree of confusion and fear. For this reason a vigil was maintained by key members of the family, food and other offerings were made, and prayers were said. The prayers included ritual invocations to the soul, repeated three times. The dead body was washed and anointed, dressed in best clothes and placed in the coffin with certain valued articles. The coffin was taken away from the place where the dead person had lived and placed in a tomb, accompanied by funeral rites and grave offerings. From the Han dynasty onwards an important tomb item was the spirit tablet placed in the tomb, which gave details of the buried person's name and status, both in life and in death. Some of these rituals, for example the invocation to the departed spirit and the offerings of food and drink, continued down into modern times.

In common with most Chinese burials Han dynasty tombs were constructed underground, their entrances concealed to deter grave robbers, and a burial mound placed over the top. There was great regional variation, with tombs being constructed from stone where local supplies permitted, or from brick or wood. The structures copied the homes of the living in their plan. They had a long ramp leading down from the surface, with main chambers on a central axis and subsidiary chambers leading off the central passageway. The vaults of the main chambers were enlarged in order to hold funeral entourages and visitors, for new funerary practices decreed that rites were now actually perfomed inside the tomb.

9
JADE BLADE MOUNTED IN
A BRONZE HANDLE (*top*)
1200–1150 BC, Shang dynasty
Length 33.4 cm
FE.21-1984
Garner Gift
商晚期銅內玉戈

JADE BLADE (*centre*)
1700–1500 BC, Shang dynasty
Length 33.5 cm
A.62-1936
商初期玉圭

JADE BLADE (*bottom*)
1200–1150 BC, Shang dynasty
Length 35 cm
A.71-1936
商晚期玉戈

The inside of Han tombs also copied houses. Pillars, rafters, tile ends and other architectural details were reproduced in brick or stone. Shown here (*10*) are three ceramic bricks which probably formed parts of the doorways of three different tombs. They have been mounted to give an impression of what such a door-frame could have looked like. They were made from baked clay, and just like pots would have been fired in kilns. The panel on the left is decorated with a stamped design of a boar and tigers. The one on the top shows trees, tomb doorways and tethered horses, while the one on the right shows figures with captions that tell us that they are officials in charge of guarding the tomb doors.

Each brick is a long, hollow, four-sided construction with openings at either end. Their construction was complex, and could have been carried out in two different ways. The first involved the manufacture of four slabs to form the sides, each slab having been rolled out on boards cut to size. The even depth of the clay walls and shrinkage cracks indicate that the clay was in fact rolled rather than pressed out. These four slabs would have had their designs stamped into them, and would then have been sandwiched between two boards to maintain an even thickness. This sandwiching resulted in some flattening of proud areas of the design, which can still be observed. The four slabs would then have been transferred to a four-sided mould, and the resultant hollow interior would have been reinforced with wet clay. The length of the square brick together with the size of the openings at either end allowed a human arm to reach all the interior surfaces. The uneven dollops of wet clay used to strengthen the interior joints are clearly visible, and imbedded in the clay are numerous potters' fingerprints. The second possible method of construction is similar to the first, except that the four slabs of clay would have been assembled round a solid central structure composed of several wooden blocks, which projected at the ends and could have been tapped out when the brick was dry. The interior surface would then have been reinforced.

The ceramic body of the bricks was analysed using a scanning electron microscope, which gave a clear picture of the structure of the clay. This proved that the bricks were made from a soil called loess, a fine, wind-borne dust blown into China by prevailing winds from desert regions of Central Asia. Loess has been deposited in large areas of north China over millenia, and in some regions is many tens of metres deep.

10

THREE CLAY BRICKS
Mounted to give an impression of the doorway to a tomb
206 BC–AD 220, Han dynasty
Lengths 110 cm (*left*), 130 cm (*top*), 120 cm (*right*)
A.13-1924, A.27-1953, A.28-1953
漢陶墓磚（三）

Another architectural item is the stone slab taken from the wall of a tomb (*11*), which came from a region with plentiful supplies of suitable stone. The style of the decoration, carved in very low relief, makes it likely that this region was Shandong province in eastern China. The designs resemble those on the walls of a famous group of chapels, or offering shrines, erected between AD 147 and 168 in front of the tombs of members of an aristocratic lineage called the Wu family. These chapel walls show a degree of uniformity which suggests that there was a workshop or workshops in the area, mass-producing sculpture of this type. As with the Wu family shrine panels, the different bands of decoration on the V&A slab show fabled figures standing in profile, each with their name carved in a little box beside them, and various magical animals, birds and reptiles. So far only one of the figures has been identified, at the left of the middle register. He is Qu Boyu, one of the disciples of the historical sage Confucius, and a man renowned for his open-mindedness and honesty. The Shandong peninsula was the region where Confucius had lived and taught, and the aristocracy of this region in the Han period and subsequently were proud of their special role as guardians of his legacy.

11
STONE SLAB FROM THE
WALL OF A TOMB
CHAMBER
AD 25–220, Han dynasty
Height 98 cm
FE.74-1982
Wellcome Gift
東漢石墓壁

Jade was still an important item among Han dynasty funeral goods. The pre-eminent position of jade at that time is indicated by the discovery of the tombs of Prince Liu Sheng and his consort Dou Wan (late second century BC). The corpses were encased from head to foot in whole suits composed of over 2,000 plaques of jade, sewn together with over 1,000 grammes of gold thread. The purity of the jade, it was believed, prevented demonic possession and saved the corpse from decomposition.

The beautiful jade horse's head (*12*) is one of the Victoria and Albert Museum's most famous, as well as most controversial treasures. It was part of the private collection of Chinese art of George Eumorfopoulos (see p.242), formed at a time when a large number of forgeries were being produced for wealthy foreign collectors, eager for novelties. It has been suggested in the past that this head and shoulders, which appears to have originally formed part of a whole jade horse composed of a number of sections of the precious mineral dowelled together, is one such forgery. It closely resembles, however, other Han dynasty horse models in ceramic or metal, even down to the neck join. These would have formed part of the tomb retinues of high officials or members of the aristocracy. As yet no complete horse of jade has been discovered (although at least one other head and shoulders does exist). The progress of archaeology in China may yet confirm the existence of such a sculpture, just as it confirmed the textual record, often doubted by sceptics, of the existence of jade burial suits.

12
JADE HORSE'S HEAD
206 BC–AD 220, Han dynasty
Height 14 cm
A.16-1935
漢玉馬首

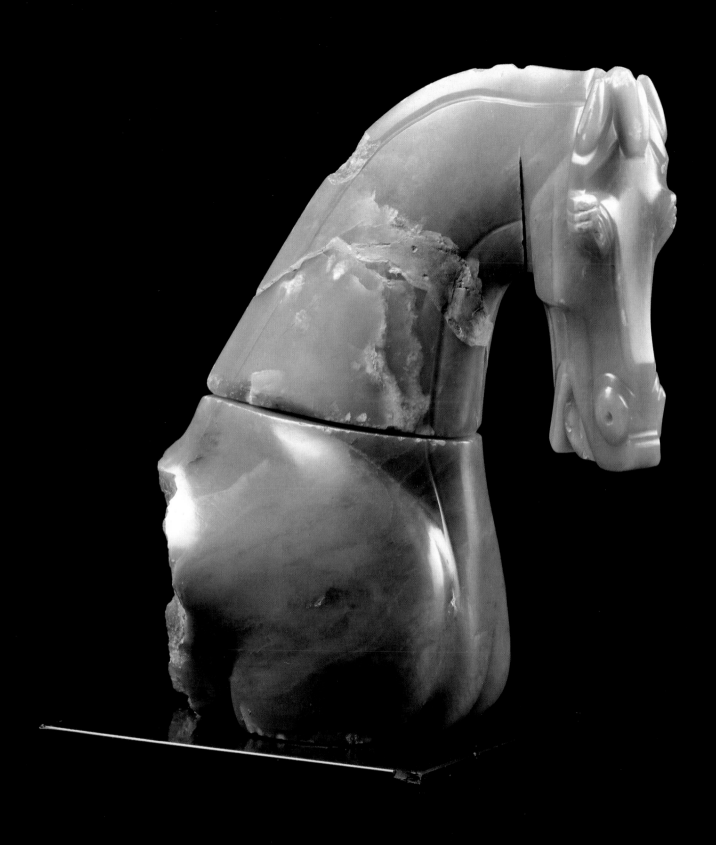

The square vase (*13*) has graceful, symmetrical designs inlaid into the surface with contrasting metals. This decorative practice became very popular towards the end of the Zhou dynasty, in the fourth and third centuries BC. At that time centres in both north and south China produced objects with abstract patterns of rhythmic curlicues. The appearance of articles such as inlaid bronzes, painted lacquers and textiles from what was known as the kingdom of Chu, a state in central southern China, was somewhat similar to that of the Victoria and Albert Museum's square vase. Those techniques of decoration continued, however, into the Han dynasty. Tombs of prominent people contained artefacts whose style of ornamentation can be compared to that of the vase. A good example is the burial of a noblewoman at Mawangdui in the north-eastern part of Hunan province, dating to about 150 BC. This remarkable site was first excavated in 1971, and it yielded not only the well-preserved mummified body of the noblewoman, but also a rich collection of finds which included painted lacquers, woven and embroidered textiles, and painted pottery. In common with other inlaid bronzes of the period, though, precious metal was used economically. Although the purple-grey patterns are inlaid silver which has tarnished, the golden patterns are actually inlaid in two layers. First, thin strips of a non-precious metal like copper were coiled closely together and hammered into pre-chiselled depressions on the vessel surface. Then, this layer was overlaid with a thin skin of gilding. The bronze vase is thus inlaid with what appears to be silver and gold. During its long history, the V&A vase has suffered spots of damage to its surface, which have been carefully filled in with beeswax coloured to look like patches of surface corrosion.

13
BRONZE VESSEL INLAID
WITH GOLD AND SILVER
About 300–100 BC,
Zhou-Han dynasties
Height 50 cm
M.1154-1926
周末 — 西漢錯金銀銅壺

We have already seen how important the provision of animal and human tomb figures was as part of the tomb retinue. Illustrated (*14*) are the figures of a dog and a serving woman. The dog is of an indeterminate but ubiquitous breed. You can still see dogs with tails curling up on top of their backs guarding country farms in China today. The serving woman wears a full-length belted robe that crosses over in front. The sleeves are cut long, so that she can tuck her hands inside them like a muff. The robe was originally painted with bright colours to show its embroidered or woven patterns; some of the colour still remains.

The Tang dynasty lasted from 618 to 906. Many Tang dynasty tombs were lavishly decorated with murals that echoed the luxurious lifestyles of their occupants. Groups of musicians, dancers and servants are thus depicted, the details of their hairstyles and clothing providing insights into the fashions of the times (see p.130). Tomb figurines afford similar interest, and the group of female attendants or dancers dating from the first half of the eighth century (*15*) are wearing high-waisted dresses typical of the early Tang period. Round their shoulders are draped long stoles. It is worth remarking that while the dress of all eight figures is very similar, almost like a uniform, their hairstyles are elaborate and varied. Some wear single and some double chignons, tied right on top of their heads with twined ribbons or cords.

Thanks to securely datable tomb excavations, we are able to trace a general progression of women's dress and hairstyles for the Sui (581–618) and Tang dynasties. By the end of the period a fuller female figure clothed in garments falling in folds and complemented by an altogether looser coiffure was fashionable, whereas earlier a slimmer silhouette was considered more beautiful. Sui dynasty ladies seem to have preferred high waistlines. These continued right through the Tang period. The top of the full-length skirt is sewn into a band which circles the body at armpit level. Sometimes the band itself or an extra sash over the waistband has long streamer ties knotted at the front. Tucked into the skirt is a low-necked top with long narrow sleeves. The neck shape varies and can be scooped, plunging, heart or V-shaped. During the Tang dynasty a fitted short-sleeved jacket appeared and this can be seen worn by the group of lady performers. Diaphanous stoles are commonly seen on such figures. We can imagine that great play was made with these long floating scarves and there were certainly many ways of draping, tucking and tying them. Apart from some skirt sections, the surviving evidence for all these styles is secondary as there are no actual complete garments to show us the pattern cut or seam arrangement.

The richly-dressed man (*16*) is a model of a senior official or courtier, from the tomb of a wealthy person. Details of his dress are not glazed like that of the female musicians, but simply painted onto the body of the clay. The figure was built up like a pot using coils of clay which can still be clearly seen inside, although the outside has been smoothed off. Drag marks from a smoothing tool are visible on the lower garments. The whole body was painted with a white kaolin ground colour, and on top of this the flesh portions were coloured a natural pink. Fine details of the features, hair and whiskers can be seen. Most interesting are the man's patterned silk robes, painted in shades of red, pink, black and green with gilding. The robes were once very brightly coloured, but tones like the pink have faded greatly; originally it would have been a deep rose colour. His shoes with their long, upturned toes and his high, cloth, official cap contribute further insights into Tang dynasty clothing fashions.

Tang tombs were richly decorated, with ornate painted roofs and lively murals. Burials contained all sorts of different items, because at this time China was very open to the outside world. Traders travelling up and down the Silk Routes (see map p.18) brought back goods from abroad, and foreign ways of making and decorating things. People from other lands were often seen, and their strange appearance and clothing fascinated the Chinese. The trade in horses from Central Asia reached its peak. All these factors are reflected in the grave goods of the Tang dynasty.

16
TOMB FIGURE (*right*)
Earthenware with painted decoration
675–725, Tang dynasty
Height 104.2 cm
c.879-1936
唐初彩陶文士俑

Some of the ceramic pieces illustrated (*17*) are made of under-fired earthenware. Shown here in the centre is a jug with a dragon handle and spout; on the right, a small pillow; and a dish with three feet on the left. During the flourishing years of the first half of the eighth century when these vessels were manufactured, great advances were made in various handicrafts like ceramic-making, textiles, paper-making and block-printing. The influence these handicrafts had on one another can be seen in plate (*17*). For example, the form and incised decoration of the dish reflect metalwork, while the splashed glazes on the dish and pillow suggest textile tie-dyeing or batik. The soft bodies were twice-fired, the second time with a layer of lead glaze. Vessels like these would not have been used for eating and drinking, because their bodies are semi-porous and easily chipped and broken. Many of them have been found in the tombs of high-ranking people in China, suggesting that they were made especially for burial. They were also exported, however, to several destinations outside China and copies of them were made in Japan and the Near East.

Two magnificent horse models (*18*) attest to the passion of the Chinese for beautiful pure-bred animals from the West. It was the Emperor Wudi of the Han dynasty (reigned 140–87 BC) who had first sent expeditions into Central Asia to fetch back 'blood-sweating' horses. The emperor believed that these 'dragon mounts' would carry him safely to paradise. Emperors of the Tang dynasty kept special stables and parks for their horses, which occupied large tracts of land around the Tang capital Chang'an (present-day Xi'an in Shaanxi province). Important tombs were sure to include models of these desirable animals. An example is the tomb of Princess Yongtai of the imperial family; she died in 701 and her grave lies a few miles north-west of Xi'an. This unfortunate princess died at the age of nineteen, ostensibly in childbirth. Another version states that she was flogged to death, or forced to hang herself, on the orders of her grandmother, the fearsome Empress Wu (who held power from about 650–705), because of an offence reported to the Empress in conversation. After the Empress Wu's death Yongtai's father ascended the throne and accorded his daughter a grand burial, re-uniting her with her husband who had died with her. Whatever the truth of Yongtai's end, we know that in burial she was surrounded by a vast army of ceramic figures; 777 unglazed and painted ones (see *16*) were excavated, along with sixty glazed soldiers, servants, huntsmen, courtiers, camels and horses.

17
DISH (*left*)
Earthenware with coloured lead glazes
700–750, Tang dynasty
Diameter 28.4 cm
C.33-1965
Maxwell Brownjohn Bequest
唐中期鉛釉陶盤

EWER (*centre*)
Earthenware with coloured lead glazes
700–750, Tang dynasty
Height 29 cm
Circ.57-1935
唐中期鉛釉陶壺

PILLOW (*right*)
Earthenware with coloured lead glazes
700–750, Tang dynasty
Length 12.5 cm
C.644-1921
唐中期鉛釉陶枕

18 (*overleaf*)
TOMB FIGURES
Earthenware with coloured lead glazes
700–750, Tang dynasty
Maximum height 74.1 cm
C.51, 50-1964
Solomon Gift
唐中期鉛釉陶馬

A common feature of many cultures is the reproduction of precious vessels in cheaper materials. Such reproductions were especially useful for burial, when the family of the deceased wished to make a fine show without squandering money. In Tang and Song China (618 to 1279), imitations of vessels made of precious metals like gold and silver were commonly made in ceramic. The mastery of the Chinese over most aspects of ceramic technology meant that they could copy almost anything. Ceramics were also less likely to lure tomb robbers, who not only denuded graves of goods but also despoiled these sanctified sites and disturbed the spirits of the ancestors. A group of silver cups and bowls demonstrate their influence on white and green ceramic vessels (19).

19

STEMCUP (*left*)
Stoneware with green glaze
550–650, Six dynasties-Tang dynasty
Height 7.6 cm
C.5-1933
左：六朝 — 唐初青釉瓷高足杯

LOBED SILVER DISH (*centre*)
With gilt fish motif inside
675–750, Tang dynasty
Length 18.8 cm
M.35-1935
中：唐初 — 中期銀碗

CERAMIC DISH (*back left*)
Yue ware
875–950, Tang dynasty-Five dynasties
Diameter 11.1 cm
FE.34-1974
Clark Gift
後：唐 — 五代越窰瓷碟

SILVER DISH (*back right*)
800–900, Tang dynasty
Diameter 12 cm
M.37-1935
唐晚期銀碗

SILVER STEMCUP (*front*)
675–750, Tang dynasty
Height 5cm
M.31-1935
前：唐初 — 中期銀杯

WHITE PORCELAIN STEMCUP (*right*)
618–700, Tang dynasty
Height 7.6 cm
C.138-1965
Seligman Bequest
右：唐初白瓷杯

During the Song and Yuan periods (960–1368) complex ritual was more often associated with male burial. Many women were simply buried alongside their husbands, in grand tombs devised for the men. Sometimes one partner could remain unburied for years, awaiting the death of the other. Chinese ideas about the complimentary nature of all components of the universe, which were either *yin* or *yang*, held that everybody should marry and that partnerships should continue into the afterlife. The concept of the negative and positive principles *yin* and *yang* is fundamental to Chinese philosophy. The words originally meant the dark and bright sides of a sunlit bank, but the concept developed to include the earth, darkness, quiescence and female values for *yin*, and heaven, light, vigour and male qualities for *yang*. It was the tension between these opposing forces that balanced the universe, and any disturbance had the gravest consequences.

Tombs from the Song and Yuan dynasties were built from a wide variety of materials according to local supplies. For example, in south-west China elaborate tombs constructed from blocks of red sandstone have been excavated, while in the northern city of Peking brick was used. The stone carving shown here (*20*) was one of a series of slabs used to line the walls of a tomb. The stone used was a white marble with a large crystal size. The calcium carbonate crystals are large enough to be seen with the naked eye and the structure of the marble is comparable with that of Greek pentelican marble. The slab almost certainly came from the north of China, as revealed by the costumes worn by the figures, and the tent depicted in the lower scene, which resembles the modern Mongol *yurt*. These, together with the evidence of a complete tomb lined with such slabs which was excavated in the north-western province of Gansu, make it likely that the slab was executed in the territory of the Jin dynasty. This was the state established by the Jurcen, a different ethnic group from the majority Han Chinese population, ruling over much of north China from 1115 to 1234. When complete, the set of slabs probably showed a cycle of stories often known in later periods as the 'Twenty-four Exemplars of Filial Piety', a popular group of Confucian tales exemplifying the lifelong duty of people towards their parents. It was at this period that this set of tales was being systematized and popularized, and it was a frequent source of motifs for tomb decoration. Support for the value system of Confucianism was always important to ruling groups who were not themselves Han Chinese, as they sought to stress their legitimacy as holders of the Mandate of Heaven.

20

MARBLE SLAB FROM THE WALL OF A TOMB CHAMBER

Jin dynasty (1115–1234)
Height 124 cm
A.59-1937
金大理石墓壁

The insides of tombs were richly decorated with carved and painted designs, and filled with a wide variety of funerary objects. The glazed pottery coffin (21) has carved designs which include the names of the guardian spirits of the Four Directions and a cyclical date. The spirits of the Four Directions, which had formed part of the decorative scheme of coffins from as early as the Han dynasty, and which continue to be used as protective decorations in tombs, are as follows; the Dark Warrior of the North (often represented by the device of a snake entwined round a tortoise), the Green Dragon of the East, the Vermilion Bird of the South, and the White Tiger of the West. The cyclical date is a product of the Chinese lunar dating system, in which a set of ten celestial 'stems' is put together with twelve earthly 'branches' to produce a combination which can recur only every sixty years. When this system is used in conjunction with the reign-period of an emperor it is unambiguous, but when it is used alone (as here) it can provide a number of alternative dates for an object, within a band determined by analysis of its style or method of manufacture. On this coffin, the date is most likely to be construed as 1206, 1266 or 1326. It was made to contain the ashes of a humble person, for it is roughly constructed, decorated and glazed. Its place of manufacture within China cannot be determined. Cremation was not a native Chinese tradition, but only entered the country with the coming of Buddhism. The practice spread gradually from Buddhist monks to the wider population of lay believers, and was most widespread in the Song period. This was despite the abhorrence of Confucian moralists, to whom the destruction of the body, given by one's parents, was a supreme act of unfilial ingratitude.

21
COFFIN FOR ASHES
Stoneware with designs carved through brown glaze
With cyclical date of 1206, 1266 or 1326, Song-Yuan dynasties
Height 28 cm
C.627-1920
Winkworth Gift
宋 — 元釉瓷骨灰棺

Another practice current in Song China, particularly in the south, was the inclusion in tombs of rice offerings for the souls of dead people. Such offerings were contained in jars (*22*), which were placed in pairs in the tombs of the wealthy. Shown here are three single burial jars, all originally forming halves of pairs. The jar on the left has a modelled relief decoration of the Green Dragon of the East; the other half of the set would have had the White Tiger of the West. The tall jar in the centre is one of a still-surviving pair, both of which are in the Museum's collection. It again bears the Green Dragon of the East, together with figures of the sun god and star gods, and cranes, the birds of long life. These two pieces have a bird on the top of their lids, a depiction of the Vermilion Bird of the South. The offering jar on the right, somewhat earlier in date than the other two, has a simple carved pattern of lotus petals and buds. This decoration may also have meaning, for it is linked with Buddhist beliefs about rebirth in the Western Paradise.

22 (left to right)

FUNERARY JAR FOR
GRAIN OFFERINGS
Longquan ware
1128–1279, Southern Song dynasty
Height 25.5 cm
C.28-1935
南宋龍泉窰釉瓷谷倉

FUNERARY JAR FOR
GRAIN OFFERINGS
Qingbai ware
1250–1350, Song-Yuan dynasties
Height 63.5 cm
C.225-1912
宋 — 元青白釉瓷谷倉

FUNERARY JAR
Yue ware
960–1100, Northern Song dynasty
38.1 cm
C.1385-1924
北宋越窰釉瓷罐

Many of the ceramics used in Chinese tombs are now viewed by collectors and museums as being rare treasures in their own right. This is true of the porcelain vase (*23*), originally a lidded jar for storing alcohol. It is painted in underglaze cobalt blue, a new technique of ceramic decoration at the time of its manufacture in the Yuan dynasty (1279–1368). Two other new cultural forms were also involved in the production of this piece. These were the use on ceramics of figurative scenes produced by woodblock printing, taken from illustrations of popular fiction and drama. The other form was the drama itself, and in particular the mixture of declamation, singing and acrobatics called *zaju* in Chinese. The centre of this art was in the city of Peking, which under the Mongol Yuan emperors became for the first time the capital of the entire empire. The play illustrated here is *The West Chamber*, China's finest love story, which has inspired countless imitations and which has remained part of the dramatic repertoire to the present day (see p.24). The story goes back to a prose tale of the Tang period, but it was retold in its present form by Wang Shifu of Peking in the thirteenth century. It tells how the talented but impoverished scholar Zhang meets the beautiful Cui Yingying while she is staying with her mother in a lonely monastery. The mother, Madame Zheng, opposes a marriage, but a clandestine liaison develops, egged on by Hongniang, the vivacious, meddling maid servant. When a furious Madame Zheng learns of the affair, scholar Zhang is despatched to the capital to seek literary success, returning in eventual triumph to claim his bride. On the side of the vase illustrated, Madame Zheng threatens Hongniang with a beating as she tries to discover the truth about her daughter's relationship with scholar Zhang, while the distraught maid buries her face in her hands.

The popular nature of the subject matter means that this object might have been thought vulgar by members of the traditional scholar ruling class. Wine jars decorated in underglaze blue with scenes from drama have, however, been excavated from tombs (where this shape of bellied *meiping* or 'prunus vase' may be particularly prevalent), including the tomb of one of the rough soldiers who helped the first Ming emperor to drive the Mongols from China.

23
VASE
Porcelain with decoration in underglaze blue
1320–50, Yuan dynasty
Height 35.9 cm
C.8-1952
元青花瓷瓶

The last period of Chinese history from which burial customs are illustrated in the gallery and this book is the Ming dynasty (1368-1644). After this time, much of the elaborate paraphernalia accompanying burial was discontinued. People were no longer entombed surrounded by the things which they had used in everyday life. Instead, paper replicas of goods needed in the afterlife were burnt at funerals. This practice continues today. Already in the Ming period wealthy people were buried in a more modest style, although the emperors continued to build massive tombs for themselves and to fill these tombs with sumptuous goods.

Tomb figures, such a common feature of earlier burials, were only used by those serving as officials to represent the large retinue which would have accompanied them in life. Three figures from the retinue of a Ming official are shown (24). They were probably made in north China, and have the same bodies and lead glazes as figures dating from the former dynasties of Han and Tang. Comparison reveals their contrastingly small size and simple characterisation.

From this brief account it can be seen that rituals of burial and the provision of grave goods were extremely important. The Chinese believed that the dead became ancestors, and ancestors had their own needs in the afterlife. Long after death the ancestors continued to be part of the family, and were cared for and propitiated. Certain days are still set aside today in the traditional Chinese calendar for these duties, the most important being *qing ming* 'clear and bright', a lunar date corresponding to early April when graves are tended.

24
THREE FIGURES FROM A TOMB RETINUE
Stoneware with green lead glaze
1500–1600, Ming dynasty
Maximum height 21.6 cm
C.149, 148, 150-1913
明中 — 晚期釉瓷侍史俑（三）

A Daoist ceremony
Illustration to Chapter 67 of the novel
< 金瓶梅詞話 > *Golden Lotus*
(1618)

Temple and Worship

CHINESE religious beliefs are varied and complex and have changed much over time, but at their heart is an idea of the continuation of life through the family line. The living venerate those who have already died, back through the generations. This belief is sometimes characterised in English by the over-simple term of 'ancestor worship', and has been a feature of Chinese society from at least as early as the Bronze Age. While other faiths developed in later times, the veneration of ancestors continued to be observed by all sections of society. The emperor himself had a special temple in his palace where he performed rites to honour his ancestors; indeed, it was believed that his mandate to rule was conferred by heaven and approved by the ancestors.

Another aspect of early Chinese worship was the veneration of natural phenomena like the sun, moon and sky. Although the actual form of the earliest Chinese religious practices is still being debated, one can say that it was an amalgam of nature worship, animism and homage to ancestors. Special places were set aside for worship, a concept that later took the form of sites for religious temples.

From the Han dynasty (206 BC–AD 220) to the early twentieth century, Chinese belief was dominated by three main religions: Confucianism, Daoism and Buddhism. Confucianism and Daoism were based on philosophical systems which incorporated ancient Chinese ideas, while Buddhism was a religion imported from India. Later Chinese Buddhism, however, transformed itself to encompass many traditional beliefs. Indeed, the boundaries between the popular religious practices of Daoism and Buddhism are much less precise than one might expect, and the appearance and lay-out of their temples are very similar.

Confucius was a moral philosopher who lived from 551 to 479 BC. He propounded ideas which evolved into a code of ethical behaviour that has governed the lives of Chinese people right down to the present day. Although there were temples to Confucius in Chinese towns, it is debatable whether Confucianism can truly be termed a religion.

The teachings of Confucius encouraged a hierarchical system of mutual obligation, whereby the relationships between the dominant and the dominated (for example ruler and subject, father and son) were strictly observed. The ancient veneration of ancestors fitted neatly within this system. Formalised ancestor worship was celebrated at all levels of society, from elaborate ceremonies at court down to makeshift altars erected in people's homes. One group of objects that illustrates this form of home worship comprises the formalised portraits of dead forbears. These ancestor portraits were displayed together with offerings to the spirits of dead members of the family, and were only brought out on special occasions like New Year and birthdays. They were expensive to commission, and were therefore mainly produced for wealthy and aristocratic households.

Depictions of the dead as they were during life, in the form of tomb murals and decorations on grave goods, are known from at least the Han dynasty. The earliest surviving ancestor portraits in the form of paintings, however, date to the Ming dynasty (1368–1644) and many examples of Qing dynasty (1644–1911) date are known. The V&A has several ancestor portraits, the finest of which (25) are a pair dating to the period 1700–1800. They show a military official and his wife, and we can tell from the badge on the man's robe (which shows a mythical animal called *qilin*) that he belonged to the second military rank in the nine-rank system. Today, the ancestor portrait has been replaced by photographs in many homes.

Daoism started as a system of thoughts and ideas which developed from about 500 BC. This 'philosophical Daoism' marvelled at the greatness of the universe and in what lay beyond it. It aimed to harmonise the inner spirit with nature, under obedience to cosmic law. This was achieved by understanding the *dao* or 'way' of the universe and by identifying thought and action with the *dao*. Many Daoist texts were written, some of which are beautiful but difficult to interpret. The most famous Daoist text is the *Dao De Jing* ('The Way of Virtue'), probably compiled in the period 400–200 BC. This extract gives a flavour of its contents:

> Vast and deep are the Nine Heavens
> Shining and wonderful the Most High
> Mysterious and ineffable the shining light of the gods.
> Shining and clear is the pure Void
> Blessed are they who ascend to the regions of silence
> Eternal life comes to them who do not lose heart.
> *Dao* is attained by those of unconquerable will.
> By stilling the emotions they achieve perfection
> They who inhibit the life force degrade their bodies
> But whoever holds to their essential being will flourish to old age.

About 250 BC these ideas were amalgamated with other beliefs which had as their goals the maintenance of health and vigour and achieving immortality. This new 'religious Daoism' had saints and deities, and was administered by priests. Popular religious Daoism believed in magic, miracles and alchemy. It became, and remained, one of the most broad-based religions of China.

The wide-ranging nature of popular Daoism is exemplified by such deities as Guan Di. Guan Di, which means 'Emperor Guan', was a title bestowed in 1594 upon a god who was originally a real person called Guan Yu. Guan Yu was an heroic and loyal soldier who fought in the civil wars of the second to third centuries AD. He was later worshipped as god of war, protector of the empire and patron of merchants and scholars. He became one of the most popular Chinese gods, worshipped everywhere in private homes as well as in temples dedicated to him. By the time of the Qing dynasty every town in China had its own 'Guan Di Temple'.

Shown here is a carved wooden temple figure, its surface lacquered over a layer of gold leaf to resemble patinated bronze, the style of representation corresponding to the late Ming or early Qing period (26). Like many religious images it contained votive gifts and scriptures in a cavity carved into the back. The figure may represent Guan Di, for it resembles other images made of porcelain and metal which have been identified as Guan Di. The group of hidden finds, however,

25 (previous pages)
PAIR OF ANCESTOR
PORTRAITS
Watercolours on silk
1700–1800, Qing dynasty
183.5 × 112 cm
(Man) E.362-1956 (Woman) E.363-
1956
清中期遺像圖絹本著色掛幅（二）

26 (right)
TEMPLE FIGURE
Wood with lacquer over a layer of
gilding
1600–1700, Ming-Qing dynasties
Height 120 cm
A.7-1917
Sandeman Gift
明一 清初漆金雕木關帝

應以天大將軍身得度者即現天大將
軍身。而為說法。

suggests a connection with Buddhism, as they comprise the following: a Buddhist block-printed book of scriptures, the 'Guanyin Sutra', dated to 1656; another text associated with Guanyin dated to 1639; a piece of gold foil; a small block of silver; a seed pearl; plants used to make medicine and incense, including an aromatic rhizome of ginseng, a piece of gum-resin, pieces of tree-fern and dried flowers; and food offerings of beans and rice grains. These offerings do not rule out the possibility of the figure being Guan Di, for they may demonstrate the syncretic nature of popular religious worship at that time. On the other hand they may indicate that the figure is in fact Buddhist, one of the Four Heavenly Generals placed to guard the doors of Buddhist temples. In the Qing period the Generals were distinguished by their accoutrements; this figure has lost any equipment it may once have carried. It is suggested that the identification of Guan Di given to other similar images should be re-examined.

Temple images in China were often dressed in real clothes. The silk robe illustrated (27) was for a Guan Di statue. It was made about a century later than the wooden sculpture just described, in about 1790. Woven into the robe are many

Buddhist text, dated 1656 (*left*)
From A.7-1917

27 (*right*)
ROBE FOR A TEMPLE
STATUE OF GUAN DI
Woven silk
About 1790, Qing dynasty
161.5 × 195.6 cm
T.752-1950
清中期關帝織錦袍

of the symbols seen on emperors' yellow clothes of the same period (see p.186). This is because Guan Di, 'Emperor Guan', was considered to be equal to a real emperor. The robe is one of a set, and would have been changed for a garment of different colour according to the season. Image robes are usually either too big or too small for a human being to wear although sometimes it is difficult to distinguish them from theatre costumes or children's clothes. They have ties rather than buttons to close them and if their linings survive these are cotton or hemp, forming a protective layer between the silk and the wood or metal of the statue. As with many secular garments, this robe has a vertical seam down the centre. Apart from the decoration around the neck, the motifs are placed symmetrically across this seam. The symmetrical arrangement is only approximate, however, and this probably indicates different weavers at work on each length of silk.

The priests who attended to Daoist temple ritual, performed ceremonies at funerals and used their arts to cast spells, cure the sick and cast out evil spirits, were important people. This is reflected in the sumptuous costumes they wore. Shown here is an embroidered silk robe of the period 1650–1700 (*28*). It is simply tailored, and is made up of lengths of material seamed together vertically and then folded in half horizontally to form the shoulder line. A broad yellow border was added round the edge and the garment was left open at the front. The garment is technically sleeveless, with an expanse of silk projecting over the edge of the shoulders to cover the arms. It is lavishly embroidered with nearly 350 Daoist figures. They are Immortals and higher gods, some with their names written beside them. The three main figures are the Jade Emperor, the Mystic Jewel and a deified form of the Daoist philosopher Laozi, known collectively as 'The Three Pure Ones'. The embroidery has been finely executed and was carefully planned. The placing of each figure within the whole presupposes a draft carried out by a designer familiar with the painted paradise scenes of which this is reminiscent. In places where the embroidery stitches have worn away over the years, the outline painting of the grand design can be discerned. The embroiderer filled in the details as the needlework progressed. Whether this detail was included on a separate draft for the embroiderer to follow or whether it was left entirely to the needleworker we shall never know. We have no information about the circumstances which caused this robe to be made, neither do we know whether it was a religious or secular workshop that produced it. When the Daoist practitioner held up his arms during one of the ritualized dances, this vestment would have been seen in all its glory.

28 (*detail left and overleaf*)
DAOIST PRIEST'S ROBE
Embroidered silk
1650–1700, Qing dynasty
127 × 208.7 cm
T.91-1928
Chester Beatty Gift
清初道士綉綢袍

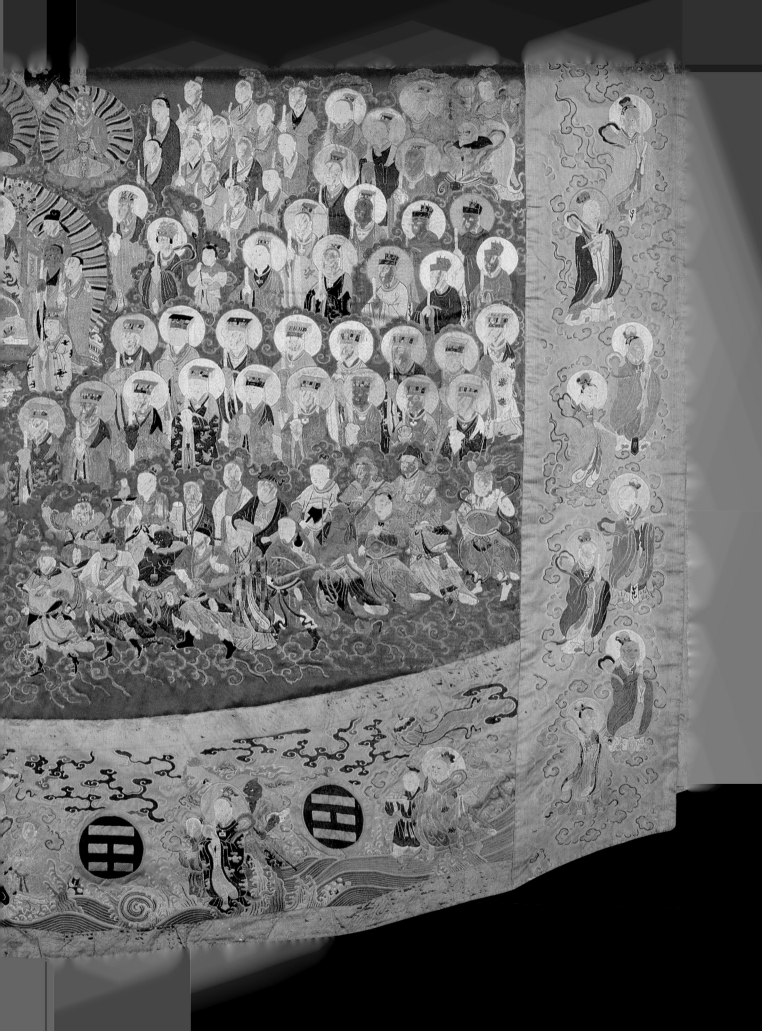

The Daoist temples in which priests officiated and people worshipped were similar in many ways to Buddhist temples. Both religions had images to worship, and in front of the images were altars for offerings. On the altars stood sets of altar vessels, which usually comprised a central incense burner with pairs of vases and candlesticks.

Shown here (*29*) are a vase from a Daoist temple on the left, and an incense burner on the right. The blue and white porcelain vase is the survivor from a pair of altar vessels. It is painted with three popular Daoist deities, star gods associated with stellar constellations and with longed-for gifts of long life, happiness and wealth. The illustrated side of the vase shows Fu Xing, star god of happiness riding a deer (whose name in Chinese represents a pun on the word for wealth) and with small boys (another lucky symbol). Overhead flies a bat, another punning symbol, this time for happiness. The long inscription written amongst these auspicious designs tells us where the vessel once stood, and when it was made. The inscription reads:

> As a willing donation to the Red Cloud Pavilion in the twenty-fifth subdivision of Donglang County in Fuzhou, Jiangxi province, I am honoured to present a pair of vases to stand for ever in front of Guansheng Dijun. A lucky day in the eighth lunar month of the forty-seventh year of Kangxi (1708).

Guansheng Dijun is another name for Guan Di, so we know that this vase came from the Guan Di Temple (the 'Red Cloud Pavilion') in the small town of Fuzhou, about 100 miles south-west of Jingdezhen. Jingdezhen was the 'porcelain city' of China where most of her porcelain was produced. On the base of the vase the name of the donor himself is revealed. He was a man called Zhou Yuan, of whom we know nothing save this one pious act.

The incense burner on the right of (*29*) was made using cloisonné enamels (see p.21). Cloisonné pieces are not so common in domestic contexts, and many of them seem to have been made for temples. A connection with a Daoist temple is suggested by the pattern in the roundels around its top. The pattern represents *yin-yang*, the two opposite but complimentary forces of positive and negative that underpin the dynamics of the Daoist universe. The other patterns of catfish with fungus, and vase with swastika containing coral, carry the hidden meanings 'may your wishes come true year after year' and 'ten thousand virtues'.

29

VASE FROM A DAOIST TEMPLE (*left*)
Porcelain with underglaze blue decoration
Dated 1708, Qing dynasty
Height 37.2 cm
Circ.699–1931
Gulland Gift
清康熙道祭青花瓷瓶

CLOISONNÉ ENAMEL CENSER (*right*)
About 1600, Ming dynasty
Height 22 cm
1489–1902
明晚期掐絲琺瑯爐

The coming of Buddhism to China during the Han dynasty was one of the great events of Chinese history, yet little is known of its early history there. Buddhism developed in India about 500 BC, and taught the suppression of passions by concentration, meditation and adherence to teaching. Its devotees stressed charity, compassion, the sanctity of life and the merit of donating worldly goods to the monastic community. They believed in karma (acts or deeds, each of which produces a good or evil result) and the evolution of the soul through a cycle of rebirths. The kernel of Buddhist moral discipline is expressed in the words of the Buddha:

Do nothing that is evil but rather do good, and purify your mind.

There are few Chinese Buddhist artefacts of Han dynasty date. Many more images and icons were produced during a great period of expansion of the religion in the sixth century AD. Two of the V&A's foremost Buddhist stone carvings were made during the sixth century, a stele (standing column) dating to 520 (*30*) and another of 544 (*31*). The earlier stele was set at the side of a road in southern Shanxi province in north China. This was done, the inscription on the stone tells us:

so that all wayfarers may gaze upon the radiant countenance, without having to turn aside their steps, and that travellers, resting themselves at this spot, may venerate the sacred images, not needing to take another path; that whether they be clergy or laity their hearts may be influenced, and whether they be monks and nuns or unordained, they may look upon this column with respectful eyes.

A group of twenty-six Buddhist believers paid for the column, which bears their names carved in rows upon its lower surfaces. The main carved decoration is of the Buddha and also of the religious debate between the Bodhisattva Manjūsri (Chinese name, Wenshu) and the pious lay believer Vimalakirti (Chinese name, Weimojie).

The monument inscribed with a date of 544 (*31*) was paid for by five donors, three of them members of the same family. It probably also stood in a public place for passers-by to worship. Like the earlier column, it probably comes from north China, in this case the borders of Shaanxi and Henan provinces.

Although some large Buddhist carvings were placed outside in public places, a larger number of images were made for temples and shrines. A central Buddha figure was often flanked by pairs of Bodhisattvas, holy beings who have escaped the cycle of rebirth to attain the ultimate state of bliss called *Nirvana*. Bodhisattvas have actually chosen to leave paradisaical bliss and come back into the world to help men. Devotional images of Bodhisattvas were understandably popular, and some Bodhisattvas attracted their own schools of worship. The small gilt-bronze image shown (*32*) was made in 534, during the Eastern Wei dynasty. It is an unusual type of image, and we know of only two such others surviving from the period. One is in the Freer Gallery in Washington DC, the other in a private Japanese collection. Both are smaller than the Victoria and Albert Museum's Bodhisattva, which also retains a good proportion of its fine gilt surface. Its inscription mentions a place called Tangxian in the province of Hebei, where this important image was probably made.

The first half of the Tang dynasty, from 638 to 845, was a time when Buddhism flourished in China. Many schools of Buddhism developed, while Buddhist monasteries multiplied and became rich in both goods and land. In 845 the reigning Emperor Wuzong, jealous of the Buddhist church's wealth and power, launched a brutal persecution which lasted for just under a year, after which the religion never regained the same level of influence at court. During its seventh and eighth century period of ascendancy the Buddhist establishment in China had retained strong links with the mother establishment in India. Buddhist monks and pilgrims, bearing scriptures and other goods, travelled in both directions down the Silk Routes (see p.18) which led out of north-western China. At the point where the Silk Routes passed Tibet to the north and entered Central Asia, a great Buddhist temple site developed at an oasis in the desert. This was Dunhuang, which flourished over 500 years, producing carving, painting and writing.

32
GILT-BRONZE
BODHISATTVA
Dated 534, Eastern Wei dynasty
Height 20.5cm
M.154-1938
東魏天平金銅鑄菩薩

About AD 1000, incursions by raiders from Tibet caused the monks to consign the incomparable library at the monastery in Dunhuang to a walled-up hiding place in one of the caves, the 'Caves of the Thousand Buddhas'. There it remained, protected by the exceptionally dry, pure desert air for over 900 years. At the beginning of the twentieth century a man called Wang discovered the hidden library, whose contents were soon dispersed. Many treasures were brought to the West, and are preserved in libraries and museums. The V&A is fortunate to curate a number of the textiles that survived. Among them are several Buddhist silk banners, two of which are illustrated here (33). Both were made between 700 and 900 AD. One is of self-patterned and plain silks and the other is decorated with resist-dyed patterns. Tie-dyeing and wax-resist dyeing methods were both used to colour early Chinese textiles but on the yellow and red banner the commonly-found technique of clamp-resist dyeing was employed. Several layers of folded thin silk were laid on a wooden board carved with a relief pattern and an identically-carved board was pressed down on top. This meant that the textile was firmly clamped at the points where the raised parts of the pattern on one board met those on the other. Dye was then poured through holes drilled in the top board and this colouring matter penetrated that portion of the silk that was not clamped. This banner has a dedicatory inscription in Khotanese brushed on the lower back which in a free translation reads, 'On the 26th day of the month *raruya* in the year of the sheep. May troubles not come near him but, as he desires [Buddhist] supreme wisdom, may all his wishes and ambitions succeed. Reverence [to the Buddhas].'

Banners like these, without figures depicted on them, were used by pious donors as offerings to honour the Buddha. They were carried aloft hooked on a staff and they also fluttered from the tops of *stupa* (domed memorial shrines). The painted wooden board across the bottom of the banners prevented the streamers becoming tangled. Inside the temple, banners were hung around the canopy and here the streamers were sometimes gracefully caught up. In this case, the weighting board helped to keep the banner in place. Additionally, thin slivers of bamboo were sewn across the banners at horizontal seams to keep the silk spread. These banners were made of very thin, almost transparent, silk so as not to obstruct what little light there was in the dim cave temples.

33
BUDDHIST BANNERS
Silk with resist-dyed patterns, and self-patterned with plain silks
700–900, Tang dynasty
Maximum length 131 cm
Ch.i.0022, Ch.00342
Stein Loan
唐中 — 晚期防染夾印紗幡

Even rarer for its completeness of preservation is a canopy made to hang over a Buddhist statue (*34*). Some of the loops which would have been used to suspend it are still intact at the canopy corners where the flaps meet the central portion. These loops may have been put through poles which were stuck in the ground. The canopy is made from hemp cloth, a strong, durable, canvas-like textile made from the fibres of the hemp plant. The botanical name of the plant is *Cannabis sativa* and it is the descendant of a wild plant which grew in Central Asia. It flourishes in poor soil and extreme weather conditions. The fibres are obtained from the centre of the stalks under the outer bark and, as with flax for linen production, these fibres must be separated from the woody parts of the plant by retting, that is by subjecting them to moisture and bacteria. They are soaked in pools for twelve to twenty-four hours and then covered with matting to ferment. A common way of making them into a continuous yarn was to knot them or glue them with saliva.

Painted in the middle of the canopy is an open lotus flower design surrounded by further lotuses in a circular and four-corner arrangement. This section would have gone immediately above the statue's head. Both the lotus and canopy were later to become two of the eight emblems particularly associated with Buddhism and these often appeared as a group on items of a secular nature also. The design on the canopy's flap-edges, which would have hung down on all four sides, is a painted rendering of a textile altar valance of a kind also recovered from Dunhuang. The only comparable pieces to the canopy so far known from this early period are a group of seventeen miniature ones, made of silk and hemp with silk tassels at the corners and held taut by means of twig frames. Even after more than a thousand years, the pinks and browns on the full-sized canopy still glow warmly.

34
CANOPY FOR A BUDDHIST IMAGE
Hemp with painted decoration
700–900, Tang dynasty
139 × 139 cm
Ch.00381
Stein Loan
唐中 — 晚期繪麻佛像寶蓋

At the same period in which these fragile textiles were produced, majestic Buddhist sculptures were being made all over China. The Buddha's head (35) is over one metre high, and is all that remains of a standing or seated statue that must have been enormous. Such an image would have been very expensive to produce, and must surely have come from an important temple. The head is cast in bronze, in sections. The sculptors who made it were extremely skilful metalworkers, for in spite of its size and the fact that it weighs over forty-five kilograms, the piece is hollow and the metal itself is only three millimetres thick. The sections are so thin and so fine that details like the lips and eyes can be traced in hollow relief inside. Traces of the core material used in casting were subjected to analysis, using thermoluminescence testing, while the head was being conserved for display. The tests confirmed the Tang dynasty date of the sculpture. Another interesting discovery was that the head was made of bronze and not iron, as was previously thought. The piece was believed to be iron because small patches of rust were seen on its surface. Tests revealed that this was because the bronze mixture contained iron and, moreover, that it is a most unusual alloy of copper, iron, tin and lead. Over the top of the bronze was laid a layer of kaolin as a ground for bright, life-like pigments used to paint the surface. This painted layer was subsequently overlaid with paper, used to repair the flaking surface of the statue and to prepare it for redecoration. The use of paper for surface repair to sculptures is a common East Asian technique. It may be significant, however, that the paper used on the Buddha's head is made from linen fibre, for this type of paper ceased to be used in China in many areas after the Song dynasty (960–1279). It therefore seems possible that the repair was an early one. Over the paper repair layer was laid a further kaolin ground, which was then painted. Conservation of the head has cleaned back to the original pigmented surface, a good amount of which is still preserved. Small areas of the paper repair and secondary painted layer have been left as a record.

35
HEAD OF THE BUDDHA
Bronze, the surface decorated in colours over kaolin ground
700–900, Tang dynasty
Height 108 cm
M.3-1936
唐中 — 晚期彩繪銅佛首

Another figure with beautiful surface decoration is the Bodhisattva Guanyin dating to the Jin dynasty, about 1200 AD (*36*). The Bodhisattva was almost certainly made for a temple in Shanxi province in north China. Guanyin is one of the most popular of all the Bodhisattvas, for his name literally means 'the one who always hears sounds', that is who listens to every prayer. For this reason Guanyin was known in China as 'the compassionate Bodhisattva', and many altars in temples were devoted to him. He was often placed behind the main Buddha image, so that the two figures stood back-to-back, separated by their altar surrounds. This Guanyin's altar surround probably took the form of a rocky grotto like the rocky throne he is sitting on. As another name 'Guanyin of the Southern Seas' shows, sailors, fishermen and others whose livelihoods exposed them to danger on the seas also prayed to the image.

Guanyin is made of blocks of wood, jointed together. Tests showed that the wood came from a Paulownia species, the 'Foxglove Tree'. The wood was then covered with a gesso ground and several layers of pigments. Extensive research on this figure when it was being conserved revealed that it had been completely redecorated at least three times (the research formed the basis for a whole book on the statue, *Guanyin – A Masterpiece Revealed* by John Larson and Rose Kerr, V&A, 1985). The original, life-like painting was laid over a base layer of gesso, composed of kaolin clay bound with animal glue. When Guanyin was first decorated about 1200 he had a brilliant red *dhōti* (skirt) with a green upper section, painted with fine gold designs. Round his shoulders was a blue stole, and his crown and jewellery were gold. His flesh was painted a natural pink colour, and his hair was blue. Later, during the Ming dynasty, the statue was repaired twice. These restorations changed his appearance completely, for the decorators sought to make him look like a gilt-bronze figure with bronze-red flesh, golden jewels and clothing, and skirt embellished with patterns in relief. This indicates a complete change in taste for sculpture, and also shows how fashions changed. Later, probably in the late nineteenth or early twentieth century, the figure was subjected to a crude repair, probably when it was sold from its temple to an art dealer. The whole surface was covered with layers of paper, which hid cracks but obscured much of the fine detail. This paper was painted with garish pigments. When Guanyin was conserved, not enough of the original painting remained, so the Ming dynasty layers were uncovered and it is this redecoration that has been preserved in the figure's appearance today.

36
THE BODHISATTVA
GUANYIN
Carved wood, the surface painted,
lacquered and gilt
About 1200, Jin dynasty
Height 114.2 cm
A.7-1935
金漆金彩繪雕木觀音

At about the same time that the V&A's Guanyin was made in north China, other distinctive figures of Guanyin were being made in the far south-western province of Yunnan. Today, Yunnan province is part of China, but in the period AD 1200–1250 it was an independent kingdom ruled by the Duan family. This was the period when gilt-bronze Bodhisattvas like that shown (37) were cast, their popularity due to the fact that they were tutelary divinities for the Duan rulers. They were regarded as a sort of dynastic talisman, and to more than one ruler actually represented the 'Luck of Yunnan'. This was because the rulers believed the image was of an Indian monk of the seventh century, who embodied the Bodhisattva during one of his lives on earth. This monk was credited with having introduced Buddhism to the kingdom.

The Guanyin illustrated opposite is a tall, slender male with broad shoulders and slim waist, dressed in the manner of an Indian Bodhisattva. His long skirt is of thin, diaphanous material which clings to the body, and is wound about with jewelled scarves. Above he is naked, save for his princely jewels; in his crown is an image of the Buddha. In style the figure shows a mixture of influences from India, Tibet, Nepal, Burma, China and south-east Asia, resulting in a beautiful and distinctive image. Such Yunnanese Bodhisattvas are rare.

37
THE BODHISATTVA
GUANYIN
Gilt bronze
About 1200–1250
Height 28.5 cm
M.155-1938
南宋金銅觀音

A wide range of Buddhist artefacts are preserved from the last two dynasties of Ming and Qing. The mid-Ming period of the fifteenth century saw the production of the painted picture, gilt-bronze image and temple vase shown here (*38, 39* and *40*). The scroll (*38*), painted on silk which has darkened considerably through exposure to the smoke of incense in a temple setting, is in fact a *mandala*, or meditational diagram, originally forming part of a set of these aids to prayer and meditation. It is executed in a style which owes much more to Tibetan (and through them, Nepalese) styles of Buddhist iconography than it does to the Chinese styles shown elsewhere in this chapter. These inner Asian styles had come to have a considerable influence on Chinese Buddhist art from the time of the Yuan dynasty, when a number of Tibetan and Nepalese monks had settled in Peking under imperial patronage. The forty-two ferocious Buddhist deities depicted are powerful protectors of true religion, shown brandishing a variety of weapons and trampling in triumph on the bodies of prostrate demons. An inscription at the bottom of the scroll dates it to the fifteenth year of the reign of the Chenghua emperor, equivalent to 1479. It was almost certainly acquired from a temple in the north-west of Peking, founded under Khubilai Khan and known in the Ming period as the *Da Long shan hu guo si*, 'Temple of Great and Mighty Benevolence which Protects the Dynasty'. This temple received particular marks of imperial favour in 1429 and again in 1472, and remained throughout the Ming dynasty a centre of Tibetan Buddhist teaching in the Chinese imperial capital, used as a lodging in the city by a number of eminent monks. The painting may well have been executed in Peking by a Tibetan monk resident in the temple. Tibetan images, particularly the gilt-bronze metalwork of the Lhasa region, remained fashionable among upper class devotees of Buddhism throughout the Ming period.

38
BUDDHIST SCROLL
Ink and colours on silk
Dated 1479, Chenghua reign period,
Ming dynasty
151 × 99.1 cm
E.61-1911
明成化佛圖絹本彩墨卷

A Tibetan Buddhist religious connection is also evident in the Ming dynasty gilt-bronze figure of a Luohan, which has an inscription in Tibetan on the front and back of its podium (39). Luohan is the Chinese name for personal disciples of the Buddha, whose depiction could perhaps be likened to that of the apostles of Jesus Christ. Sets of figures of Luohans were placed in the side chambers of temples. There were usually eighteen, although smaller and larger sets are also known; there are many temples dedicated to 500 Luohans. Each figure was represented in a very realistic manner, and some of them may have been portraits of real people. Many Luohans look like Indian or Tibetan ascetics, emphasising the facts that Buddhism came originally from India to China, and that Chinese and Tibetan monks mixed freely. The Luohan shown here looks Chinese or Tibetan, with strongly modelled features and the elongated earlobes which are a mark of holiness on Buddhist figures (see p.108). He wears the robes of a monk with hems and borders incised to look like figured silk, and holds a book of Buddhist scriptures inscribed in Tibetan. The figure is gilt all over save on the back, suggesting that it was made to be looked at only from the front. On the back is a brief inscription saying 'number 7 on the east', which indicates the original position of the Luohan in its temple chamber.

39
GILT-BRONZE OF A
LUOHAN
1400–1500, Ming dynasty
Height 50 cm
FE.104-1970
明初金銅羅漢

We have mentioned the use of altar vessels in Daoist temples, and their similarity to those found in Buddhist temples. One vase (40) in the collection at the V&A was made to contain flowers, feathers or other decorative items, for it has a ring of holes around the neck to support such things individually. Its decoration of scrolling lotus and stylised conch shells suggests that it was made for a Buddhist temple. The painted mark on the base tells us that it was produced in the mid-Ming period, during the reign of the Jiajing emperor (1522–66).

Scene in a Buddhist temple (*left*)
Illustration to the drama
< 續西廂升仙記 > *Ascent to Immortality from the West Chamber, continued* (1628–44)

40 (*right*)
VASE
Porcelain decorated with underglaze cobalt blue
Jiajing reign period mark (1522–66), Ming dynasty
Height 31.1 cm
C.100-1928
Bloxam Gift
明嘉靖青瓷瓶

The last dynasty of China was the Qing dynasty, which ruled from 1644 to 1911. Four items from this dynasty are illustrated, a woven silk picture (*41*), a Buddha (*42*) and two rugs (*43*). The woven silk picture, richly worked with threads of seven colours, wound gold thread and flat gold strip on a rich blue ground, was made between about 1740 and 1800. It shows the figure of the Bodhisattva Guanyin in yet another aspect, seated on a lotus throne and with one pair of hands pressed palms together in the gesture known as *anjali mudra*, the 'mother' of all the other esoteric gestures which played such a large part in the schools of Buddhism patronized by the imperial court. Two other arms hold a rosary and a lotus flower. This style of multi-armed image is one favoured by Qing dynasty schools of Buddhism with Tibetan affiliations.

41
BUDDHIST PICTURE
Woven silk
1740–1800, Qing dynasty
146 × 95.2 cm
T.97-1966
Seligman Bequest
清中期絲織觀音圖

Buddhism had originated amongst the followers of an Indian prince (probably 563–483 BC) who renounced his position to lead a holy and monastic life. Thus the first Buddha was a real person, and his teachings were the basis for many later holy texts. The gilt-bronze figure (42) of about 1750 is an image of Sakyamuni, the given name of the Indian prince, and depicts the climactic event of the Buddha's last life on earth. In keeping with the Buddhist belief in rebirth, Sakyamuni had already passed through several preparatory lives as a Bodhisattva, on the path of progression towards the ultimate enlightenment of Buddhahood. When he arrived at his ultimate birth, he chose as parents a virtuous couple who were king and queen of a small state in Nepal. The queen's conception was immaculate, and ten months later the boy was born painlessly from her right side as she stood grasping the branch of a tree. The tiny infant was received by gods, bathed, and immediately able to walk. Taking seven steps to the north, he stated that this was to be his last birth. His supernatural status was confirmed by sacred marks found on his body, and his subsequent intellectual and martial development was rapid. His father provided every worldly comfort, and beautiful daughters of noble families were sent for his choice in marriage. The gods, however, arranged that he should see the other side of life in the form of a sick man, a corpse and a religious wanderer, and the young man thereupon planned to renounce the world. Even the presence of his newly-born son could not hold him back. Fleeing the palace by night, he halted to cut off his long hair and beard with his sword. His hair sprang into tight curls to the right, and these are one mark of the Buddha, shown on the figure in (42). The pendant earlobes (stretched by the heavy jewellery he wore as a prince), the simple monk's robes (donned in exchange for his princely clothing) and the protruberance on top of his head (the *usnisa*, a mark of attainment of supreme wisdom) are further attributes of Buddhahood.

An intensive programme of religious study and severe fasting failed to achieve Enlightenment, so the young man sat underneath a tree and vowed not to move until he had achieved his goal. The goddess of evil tried to tempt him with beautiful maidens and hideous demons, but Sakyamuni resisted and summoned up the earth goddess to bear witness to his resistance of evil. This is the moment depicted by this image, for the figure is shown with hands in the gesture of 'calling the earth to witness', the moment before Enlightenment was attained. Naturally enough, this was one of the most important happenings in the whole of Buddhist history, and the place in India where the Buddha attained Enlightenment has been a centre for pilgrimage for more than two thousand years. That place is Bodhgaya in north-east India, and is still an active centre of worship for Chinese pilgrims today.

42
SAKYAMUNI BUDDHA
Gilt bronze
About 1750, Qing dynasty
Height 93 cm
FE.58-1977
Shaw Gift
清中期金銅佛主

We have mentioned the Buddhist faith in India, China and Tibet. Another country which developed strong traditions of Buddhist worship was Mongolia. Many Chinese Qing dynasty Buddhist objects have links with Mongolia, like the pair of carpets shown here (43). These woollen rugs were made especially to go round temple pillars, and the curling dragon design is an appropriate one for such a use. When laid out flat, the designs on rugs like these lose their coherence, and it is only when they are displayed in the way originally intended that the dragons' coils join up. Photographs of temple interiors show silk streamers as well as rugs circling pillars, religious pictures suspended from the ceilings and narrow carpet runners covering the floors. The dragon motif with scattered clouds and striped water at the bottom is a widely-used pattern in China and not one reserved exclusively for Buddhist items. This pair of rugs were presented in 1885 for use in a Buddhist temple by a Mongol noble named Burintogos. We know this from the inscription at the top of each rug in Mongol and Chinese respectively. The rug with the Chinese dedication gives a date 120 years earlier (1765), but this is thought to be a weaving error.

43
WOOLLEN PILLAR RUGS
Dated 1885, Qing dynasty
Height 193 cm, width 112 cm
T.238,239-1928
Highfield Jones Gift
清光緒柱梁氈毯

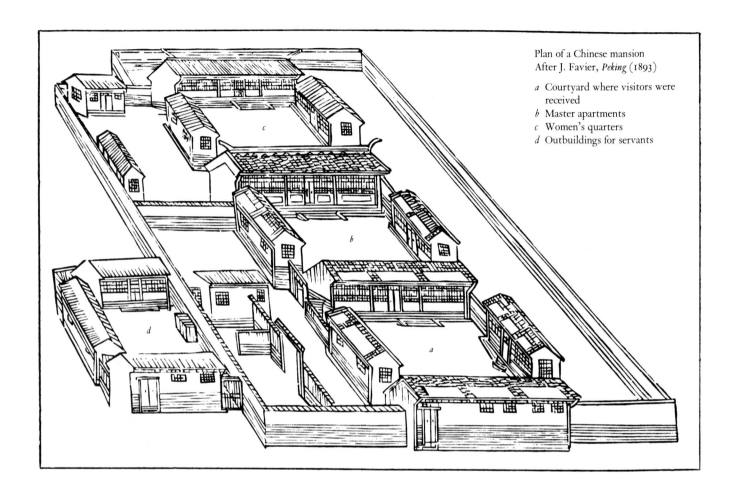

Plan of a Chinese mansion
After J. Favier, *Peking* (1893)

a Courtyard where visitors were
   received
b Master apartments
c Women's quarters
d Outbuildings for servants

Living

THE traditional-style Chinese house of the upper classes was built round a courtyard and constructed of cantilevered timber beams supported by columns. It was the home of the joint family unit, several generations and their servants living there. There were regional variations in house construction and differences dependent on each family's financial position, but from about the Han dynasty (206 BC–AD 220) the exterior aspect of most houses was established with high blank walls punctuated only on one side by the entrance gate. It was inside these protective walls that a family's taste and wealth would really be revealed.

It is the interior of the home and the furnishings inside the rooms that is the subject of this chapter. The items from Chinese houses which are now in the Museum were owned by people who lived well above poverty level. We will look at just a selection of these, dating mainly from the period 1200–1900, and also at various aspects of home life: writing, dressing and personal adornment, and celebrating. The disposition of rooms in a Chinese mansion varied, but amongst them would be reception rooms, a study or studies for the men, bedrooms and other private rooms, women's apartments separate from these, and service quarters. It is not possible to assign every object shown here to a particular kind of room although by reference to a variety of sources, notably woodblock prints, contemporary manuals of elegant living and works of literature, as well as the designs incorporated into the objects themselves, we can place some of them in their original settings.

Tables, chairs, storage chests and beds were the first requirements of all but the humblest Chinese interior schemes. Chinese furniture is found in hard and soft woods, lacquered wood and bamboo. It was placed about the rooms often against the walls and, ideally at least, in a symmetrical arrangement which reflected the social hierarchy of the rooms' occupiers. Some of the pieces had very precise uses and as such were confined to particular rooms. Many were general purpose items, moved from one room to another and taken into the garden in fine weather. They thus served a number of functions as the need arose. A table and chair are here seen (51) being used for writing but this would not have been the only way they were employed.

Chinese rooms had a lot of textile furnishings and the structure of wooden furniture was often concealed by silk drapery. Upholstery, in the sense of padding out and fixing a decorated textile semi-permanently to an item of furniture, was unknown in China. Instead, removable cushions were placed on the throne-like chairs and also on the platform beds when they were used for daytime seating. Wooden chairs with arms, at least during the Ming and Qing periods (1368–1911), did not usually have cushions on them but, on occasion, were draped with covers which hung over the back rail, down the inside back, across the seat and down the front.

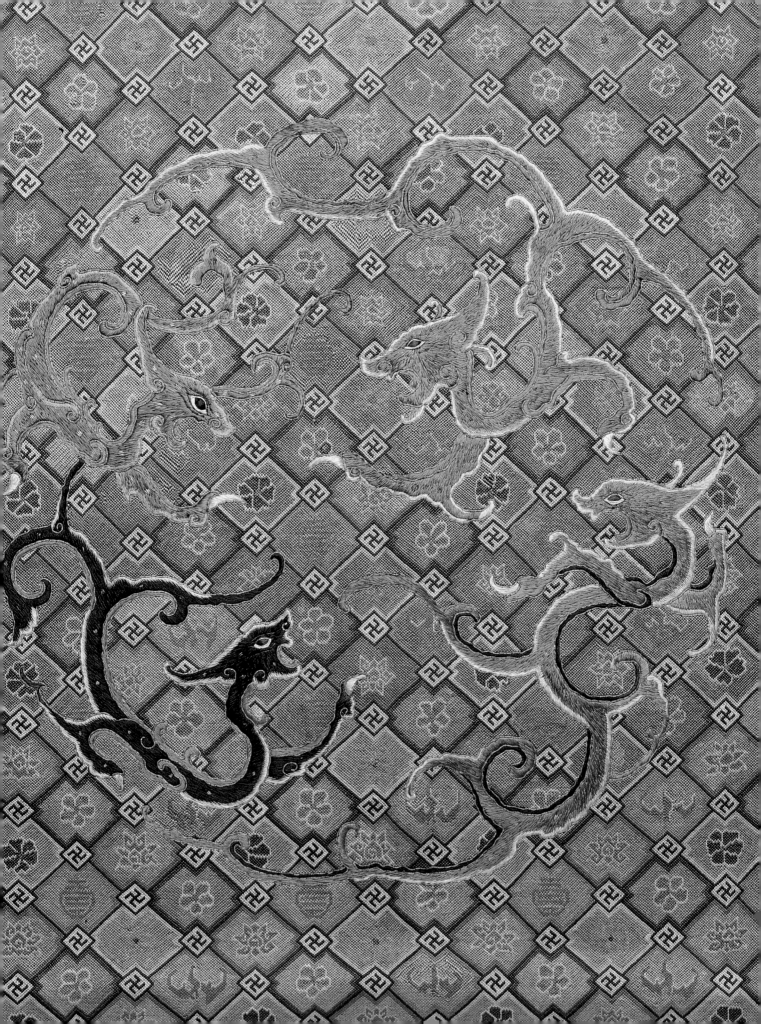

Table frontals were made to match sets of chair covers, although the Museum's embroidered frontal (44) does not today form part of such a group. It is arranged in two tiers with a narrow section of cloth overlapping a deeper length. The frontal was suspended around the front and both sides of the table, covering the legs. It did not cover the table top. The back of the table was left free so that a person could sit at it comfortably although here the textile does not quite fit the table and extends a little around the back.

Counted thread embroidery worked regularly across an even, openwork grid of gauze silk is the main technique used on this intricately-patterned frontal. Vertical stitches are used throughout and, except for the dragons on the lower section and the small roundels on the pelmet, these regular stitches cover the ground material completely. An unbroken herringbone pattern is formed by the straight stitches, and this goes right across the piece regardless of the colour changes of the embroidery thread. In addition to this underlying pattern, there is a more obvious one of diamond and octagonal lattices, each ogive containing a tiny lotus, long life character or bat. Long satin stitches and couched gold thread form the sinuous spotted dragons as well as the floral circles above them. Although there are signs of considerable wear at the top where the frontal would have been tied around the table legs with tapes, the embroidery itself has proved extremely durable. The stitching was executed with such uniform tension, a considerable achievement over such a large piece, that the frontal was not in any way distorted and, because of this, it hung straight without undue stress being placed on any one area.

Examples of Chinese velvet survive in some quantities from the seventeenth to the twentieth centuries. The earliest date that Chinese weavers first made this lustrous fabric is still being debated. We can, however, say with some confidence that the length shown here (45) dates from between 1670 and 1730. The section reproduced is one end of a 3.5 metre length, the other end having an identical design, and the middle bearing the same scrolling foliage but with a fully-opened lotus flower. There is a selvedge at either side of the cloth indicating that this represents an entire width as woven on the loom. The cut tufts of rich red velvet are interspersed with areas left free of pile and these are enhanced with several other colours including gold and silver. Similar lengths of velvet would have been joined to this one down each of its long sides forming a large rectangular cover. As such it would have been spread over a *kang*, the heated raised platform used for sitting as well as sleeping, found in northern Chinese homes.

This velvet strip was woven to suit the furnishing requirements of the Chinese mansion. The frontal was also measured, embroidered, and made up to fit a specific size of table. Yardage with a repeat pattern that was cut off the bolt as required was not used as much in Chinese as in European interiors. Self-patterned silks with small all-over designs were, on the whole, reserved for linings and facings and this is the sort of material that backs and supports the table frontal.

44 (*previous pages*)
TABLE FRONTAL
Silk embroidery
1670–1730, Qing dynasty
79.3 × 262.9 cm
FE.37-1911
清早期穿繡紗桌圍

TABLE
Huali wood
1550–1650, Ming-Qing dynasties
Height 87.7 cm
FE.21-1980
明末 — 清初花梨木桌

45 (*right*)
VELVET
1670–1730, Qing dynasty
Entire panel 340.5 × 66 cm
FE.9-1980
清初絲絨料

While the frontal and velvet *kang* cover would have retained a draped quality in use, a pair of shaped pictures (*46*) rely more on the effects of accomplished embroidery to point up their textile properties. The pictures show the 'Royal Mother of the West' with graceful fairy maids attending her. When the embroidery was first done, that is some time between 1730 and 1800, the colours would have been bolder and stronger than they appear today although the blue silk ground, a favourite colour for pictorial needlework, has not faded very much. The imaginative use of straight satin stitches executed at different angles, combined with the stitches on the clothes of the figures which give a more three-dimensional character to the work, invite the viewer's eye to linger. The shape of the pictures also holds our interest and it is likely that it echoed the shape of the furniture in the room, the entire contents of which were probably designed to order. From the 1750s onward, the moneyed élite thought it chic to put glass over the front of their pictures and so this pair might well have been glazed from the time they were first made. There is no eighteenth-century glass on them today although the wooden frames and metal hangers are contemporary with the embroideries.

It is not clear which type of room the textile pieces described above would have been placed in. They seem suited to the more public rooms. Certainly the splendid screen (*47*) would have been prominent in one of the reception rooms in a Chinese mansion. Its position may have varied according to the nature of the occasion and, having designs on both sides, it did not necessarily always stand against a wall. Dated and inscribed screens, some including names of donors, indicated that these were presentation pieces. Their brilliance and showiness verify this and the celebratory themes pictured on them identify them as lavish gifts for birthdays. Here, the scene is the popular representation of the birthday party of the 'Royal Mother of the West', *Xi Wang Mu*, who is being given the peaches of everlasting life by the Eight Immortals. The screen was produced some time between 1625 and 1650 and the technique is one peculiar to China, used during the seventeenth century and not much afterwards. The picture elements were carved through the built-up coats of dark lacquer on each wooden screen panel. Tinted lacquer and oil paints were then applied to the cut areas producing a polychromatic effect on a black ground.

46 (*right*)
EMBROIDERED PICTURES
1730–1800, Qing dynasty
64.9 × 105.4 cm
T.355-1970 and T.356-1970
清中期刺繡掛圖

47 (*overleaf*)
LACQUER SCREEN
1625–50, Ming-Qing dynasties
250.4 × 587.5 cm
163-1889
明末 — 清初雕漆屏風

A smaller screen (*48*) is fashioned from a slab of variegated slate and is worked in several layers like a cameo. The cream and green tones largely form the picture and these have been chiselled away in places to reveal a background colour of dull plum. The scene shows pavilions on the Islands of the Immortals, a magic paradise land in the Eastern Sea. Two cranes fly out of the clouds and these birds together with the evergreen pine trees growing on the island traditionally bear wishes for a long life, something to which all Chinese aspired and which also had implications for the continuation of the family line. The screen is not carved on the reverse and needs a wooden frame to hold it upright. It would have stood on a table as decoration.

Other small items which would have been placed around either the public or private areas of the house are represented here by a fruit dish and a lantern. Seasonal fruits were polished and piled in pyramids on large dishes. The celadon green dish rests on a stoneware stand (*49*): the dish was made in south China, the stand was from northern kilns, and both were made in the same century. In the evenings, wax candles inside paper, oxhorn or porcelain lanterns illuminated interiors. One such lantern (*50*) from the period 1725–50 is faceted with different lattice patterns, an effect achieved by a worker with a skilled and steady hand. The shaped openings were cut with a knife after the clay had dried for a while and before the lantern was glazed. To diffuse light across a wider area, lanterns were sometimes set on tall wooden stands, which had adjustable poles to vary the height.

48 (*right*)
TABLE SCREEN
Slate with wood stand
About 1850, Qing dynasty
Height 58.4 cm
1071-1852
清晚期石板木座插屏

49 (*overleaf left*)
DISH OF GLAZED
PORCELAIN
Longquan ware
1300–1400, Yuan-Ming dynasties
Diameter 35 cm
300-1902
Hamilton Gift
元 — 明初龍泉窯瓷盤

STAND OF GLAZED
STONEWARE
Jun ware
1300–50, Yuan dynasty
Height 22 cm
C.108-1939
元鈞窯瓷盤座

50 (*overleaf right*)
LANTERN
Porcelain with decoration painted
over the glaze
1725–50, Qing dynasty
Height 33.5 cm
C.1435-1910
Salting Bequest
清初 — 中期彩瓷燈

The study was an intermediate sphere between the reception rooms and the private apartments. Here, a gentleman might entertain a few male colleagues or spend time on his own. This room was where he would play music, paint, admire his art collection (see p.217), read or write. He might also have a bed where he would sleep when he was not with one of his wives or concubines. Plate (51) shows some of the equipment needed for writing.

This area of Chinese life was largely a male preoccupation. Scholars in China paid a lot of attention to the writing implements they had on their desks, wrote about them, and used them as signs of their literacy and refinement and as status symbols. A tapering brush was used for everyday clerical work as well as for more artistic calligraphy. Neither the hand nor the wrist of the writer touches the paper and sometimes a small stand, or wrist rest, gives support when the writer pauses. The brush is held in a vertical position. A solid ink cake or stick provides the

medium for writing, and this is dissolved into a liquid by rubbing it on a slightly hollowed-out stone containing a little water. Other accoutrements found on writing tables are pots and trays for storing brushes, droppers for pouring the water onto the stone, pots for washing brushes, saucers for testing the brushes, brushrests and paperweights. A gentleman would also possess his own seal carved with his name. He would use this like a small printing block, dipping it in red seal paste and affixing his mark to anything that needed his signature. All of these things were often made by famous craftsmen, and were treasured by their owners.

The private rooms were gender-segregated zones for the more personal routines of daily life. The bed (52) and the washstand (53) shown here would have been used in such areas. The bed is given the name 'rattan bed' or 'frame bed' by the Chinese to distinguish it from a number of other bed types such as those with solid sides and those with antechambers attached. It dates from the seventeenth century and is made from *huali*, the Chinese name for members of the *Pterocarpus* family of hardwood trees which grow in China and south-east Asia. Hardwood furniture was

51

a TABLE
1550–1650, Ming-Qing dynasties
Height 87.7 cm
FE.21-1980
明末 — 清初木桌

b CHAIR
1550–1650, Ming-Qing dynasties
Height 97 cm
FE.72-1983
Addis Bequest
明末 — 清初木椅

c VASE, *d* INKSTICK REST,
e PAPERWEIGHT *Ruyi*, *f* SEAL
BOX AND *g* THREE SEALS
Bronze inlaid with silver wire
1575–1640, Ming dynasty
Height of vase 10.5 cm
M.605(7)-1924
Royal Asiatic Society Gift
明晚期錯銀銅文具：
瓶 墨床 鎮紙如意 印泥盒 三章

h STONE FOR GRINDING
INKSTICKS
1800–1900, Qing dynasty
FE.25-1976
清晚期石硯

i RED LACQUER BRUSH
AND CAP
1580–1620, Ming dynasty
FE.48-1974
Addis Bequest
明晚期雕漆管筆

j BRUSHREST
Bronze inlaid with silver wire
1575–1640, Ming dynasty
5373-1901
明晚期錯銀銅筆架

k FLOWER POT OF GLAZED
STONEWARE
Jun ware
1300–1400, Yuan-Ming dynasties
Height 27 cm
C.35-1935
元 — 明初鈞窯瓷花盆

Bedroom scene (*overleaf left*)
Illustration to the novel
< 禪眞逸史 > *Tales of Zen and Dao*
(1621–27)

52 (*overleaf right*)
BED
Huali wood
1600–1700, Ming-Qing dynasties
Height 206 cm,
FE.2-1987
明末 — 清初花梨木床

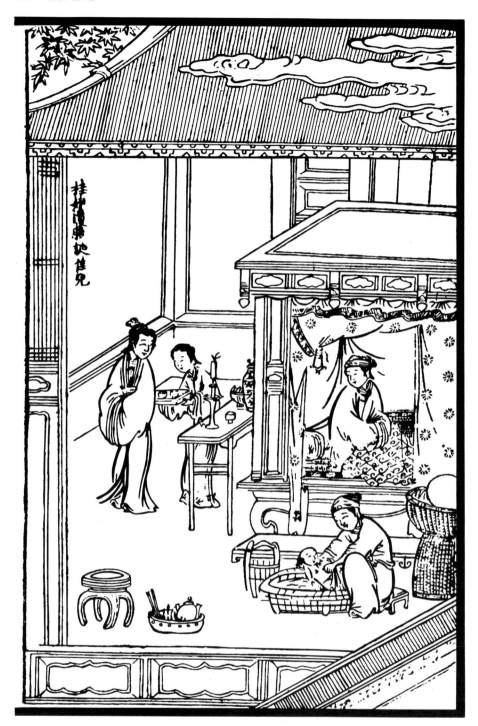

not thought as elegant as furniture of lacquered wood, but it was still used in the homes of the fairly rich.

Textiles made into curtains, pelmets and covers for quilts would have dominated the beds in a Chinese house. Many of these beds would have been massive affairs and, like the *kang*, would have been used for reclining and sitting during the day as well as for sleeping at night. Although not heated like the *kang*, they had the advantage of being raised up and this, together with the closed curtains, would have afforded some protection from draughts. Braziers and woollen pile rugs might also have been taken up onto the bed.

The wooden washstand with metal basin is attractive and superbly crafted. Like the elaborate make-up ritual discussed below, frequent washing was the preserve of the upper classes who were dependent on their servants for fetching and carrying. The tall part of the stand was used for hanging towels, and although it looks as if it might fold flat it was not, in fact, made to do so. There are known examples of folding washstands but this one is very light and could have been both carried easily and conveniently stored. The stand dates from between 1550 and 1620 and the basin from between 1650 and 1720.

The clothes in the collection of the Victoria and Albert Museum would have been worn by the rich, but even families with quite modest incomes possessed silk garments, albeit plain, for special occasions. China has had a native silk industry for centuries and so this lustrous textile has been widely available. The clothes traditionally worn by well-to-do Chinese are today called 'gowns' or 'robes' in English. The term is misleading as it suggests informal attire worn around the house for relaxation. The long garments shown here (54 and 55) would not necessarily have been worn in this way and are typical day wear of their class and respective times. Because most surviving robes are in this style and date from the Qing dynasty (1644–1911) to the Republican period (1912–49), we must not presume that the cut of Chinese clothes has always been like this. The pottery figurines from the Han and Tang periods (206 BC–AD 906, plates 14,15,16), for example, indicate a very different mode of dressing.

Whatever the current style, outward appearances played an important role in how people from the élite classes presented themselves to the world. In the Qing dynasty, women favoured highly decorated clothes with applied borders. Their robes never trailed along the ground. The bright purple long life characters on this silk embroidered robe (54) signify that it was made for an older woman. It may have been made for a birthday celebration, presented to a parent by her children. It would then have been worn on subsequent auspicious occasions to bestow longevity on the wearer.

The man's garment (55), an elegant grey velvet robe, has a repeat design of bamboo and flower sprays across its surface. It dates from a time in the twentieth century when western suits would also have been seen on the streets of Chinese cities. The older and more conservative men retained the traditional style of dressing right up to the 1949 revolution, although almost all males cut off their plaited back hair soon after the earlier revolution which overthrew the emperor in 1911. During the troubled early decades of the twentieth century there was a fusion of the old and the new, the traditional Chinese and the Western. European-style trilby hats and trousers with turn-ups as well as lace-up brogue shoes were frequently worn with this type of ankle-length robe. Before 1900, most men belted their robes. Later, perhaps because a narrower cut of robe was introduced, this was not the case. Just as the belt was disappearing as an accessory for men's robes, so the pocket started to be a feature of Chinese garments, though at first a hidden one. This side-fastening robe has a pocket sewn onto the inside flap.

53 (right)
WASHSTAND
Huali wood
1550–1620, Ming dynasty
Height 183 cm
FE.28-1989
Mrs Amy Tsui Gift
明晚期花梨木面盆架

BRASS BASIN
1650–1720, Qing dynasty
Diameter 44.9 cm
FE.19-1982
Purchased with the aid of the Friends of the V&A
清初白銅面盆

54 (overleaf left)
WOMAN'S EMBROIDERED ROBE
1870–1911, Qing dynasty
132 × 136 cm
T.231-1948
清晚期女綉綢袍

55 (overleaf right)
MAN'S VELVET ROBE
1900–30, Qing dynasty-Republic
145 × 204 cm
FE.126-1983
Addis Bequest
清末 — 民國男絲絨袍

Belts of various kinds were worn by both Chinese men and women at different times throughout the dynasties. They helped keep garments fastened, were essential accessories for men who carried swords, and added contrasting highlights to an ensemble. They were seldom used, however, to accentuate the shape of the human figure as in some other cultures. Until the Han dynasty, hooks secured belts and afterwards buckles and clasps were adopted as illustrated on the bottom row of (56). Rectangular gold foil plaques depicted on the third row were used for decorating the length of a belt, while differently-shaped ones, such as those on the top row, were sewn straight onto clothing, hats or headbands. The toggles, in the second row, were perhaps used on a drawstring to fasten silk purses, or they may have been threaded onto the end of the cord that hung down from a rigid fan to act as a counterbalance. Although purses and fans were accessories common to both sexes, these agate toggles were almost certainly used by women because they are carved in the shape of jujubes, sometimes called Chinese dates, which carry the hidden meaning 'may you soon give birth to sons'. Toggles of a different design would have been used on men's pouches that were looped on a belt or, in the twentieth century, stowed in pockets.

56

JADE PLAQUE *(top)*
1500–1620, Ming dynasty
Diameter 11.2 cm
1643-1882
Wells Bequest
明晚期玉飾

THREE AGATE TOGGLES
(second row)
1700–1850, Qing dynasty
Maximum height 6 cm
391, 392, 393-1902
Waldo-Sibthorp Gift
清初 — 中期瑪瑙墜子（三）

GOLD FOIL BELT PLAQUES
(third row)
1400–1600, Ming dynasty
Maximum height 5.7 cm
M.94(7)-1938
明金箔帶飾

JADE BELT BUCKLE
(bottom left)
1600–1700, Ming-Qing dynasties
Length 11.2 cm
FE.46-1981
明末 — 清初玉帶鉤

JADE AND METAL BELT
BUCKLE *(bottom right)*
1200–1600, Song-Ming dynasties
Length 6.8 cm
FE.126-1988
南宋 — 明玉嵌金屬帶飾

One of the personal items sometimes kept in such pouches was the snuff bottle. These endearing knick-knacks seem to have been mainly used by men, and the practice of sniffing the powdered tobacco, herb and spice mixture was established during the eighteenth century. Snuff bottles were made in a variety of shapes and materials. Three are shown here (57). The bottle on the left is made of porcelain painted in enamel colours and dates from the Daoguang reign period (1821–50). It shows a spotted deer pointing to a magic fungus with its hoof. The two other bottles are of glass and were made during the Qianlong reign period (1736–95). The bottle in the centre is delicately painted in enamels; the one on the right is inlaid with mother of pearl, lapis lazuli, jasper, amber and coral.

57
SNUFF BOTTLES
Porcelain and glass
Qing dynasty (1644–1911)
Maximum height 7.8 cm
C.1694-1910, C.1583-1910,
C.1573-1910
Salting Bequest
清瓷 玻璃鼻煙壺

Among jewellery types, female hair ornaments have been prominent Chinese dress accessories throughout the centuries (58), more so than necklaces, bracelets, earrings and rings. Women wore more jewellery than men although male bureaucrats are depicted as sporting a large array of variously-shaped hats especially from the Han to the Ming dynasties (206 BC–AD 1644). These hats denoted rank and also gave support to a man's upswept knot of hair. The jade hairpin for a man at the left of centre of illustration (58) would have been pushed through the sides of a small hat-like ornament that covered such a knot.

On the basis of archaeological evidence the other hairpins in the same picture are all thought to be for women. Their hairstyles were especially ornate, with the natural hair often supplemented with false pieces and reinforced with stiffened gauze bases. Women embellished their chignons with flowers and small plaques and these, together with the hairpins, made for very striking coiffures, the accessories showing up particularly well against shiny, dark east-Asian hair. The double-pronged pins probably held the hairstyle in place while the single-ended ones were purely decorative.

58
GROUP OF HAIRPINS

Gold, silver, jade, glass, pearl and feathers
1200–1850, Song-Qing dynasties
Maximum length 27.5 cm
M.56, 57, 58-1935, A.48-1938
M.40, 41-1935, M.128(4)-1938
宋 — 清金 銀 玉 玻璃 珠 羽毛簪

GROUP OF GOLD ORNAMENTS

1650–1900, Qing dynasty
Maximum width 5.5 cm
M.93(2)-1938, M.99-1937
清金服飾

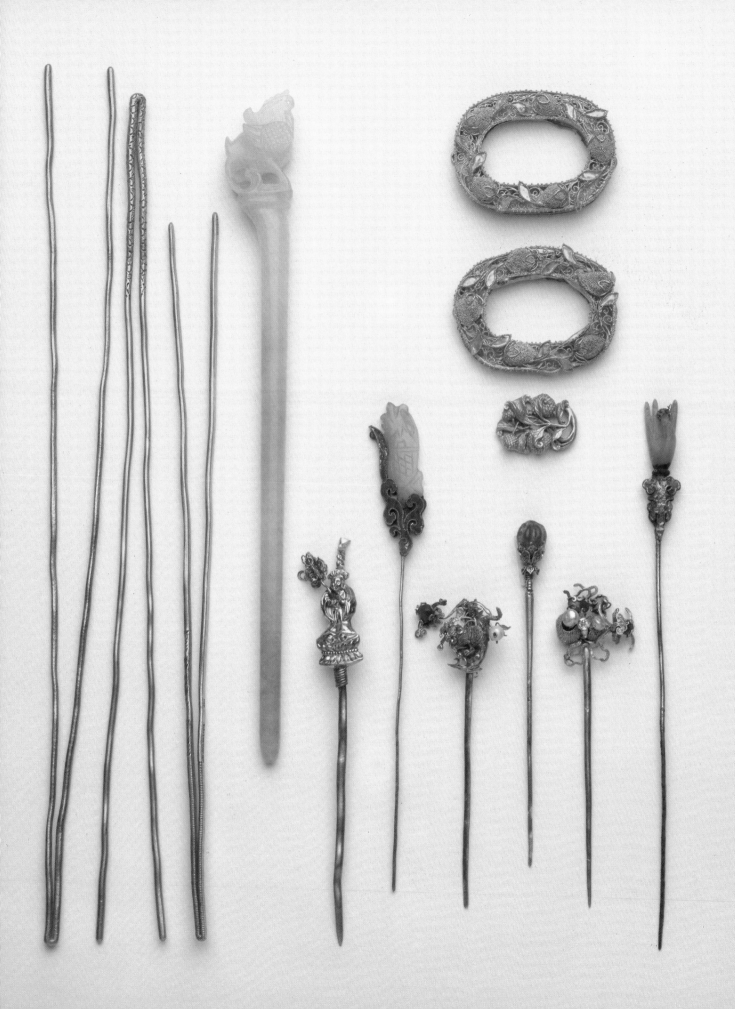

The boxes shown in plate (59) may have been used for storing jewellery, hairpins or cosmetics. Excavated silver boxes of a type similar to the two Tang dynasty examples, though undecorated, were found to contain medicinal herbs and minerals. Only rare or precious items would have been stored in boxes of silver, for together with gold it was the most expensive material. Female 'beauties' donning their finery were a conventional subject matter for Chinese painters, and such paintings feature lacquered toilet boxes similar to the Museum's example. Men are never depicted engaged in such an activity. Prior to the Qing dynasty, however, when they wore their hair in an unadorned plait down their backs, men's hairstyles were elaborately twisted and braided, requiring some form of pomade and as many securing pins as a women's coiffure. We should not discount the possibility of the lobed and tiered lacquer box having been owned by a man, as nothing assigns it to one gender rather than the other.

This is not the case, however, with the small jade box on the left in plate (60). We are now beginning to understand which items would have been made for and used specifically in the women's apartments, by virtue of the designs on them. The symbolic content of these designs is redolent of those domestic concerns thought to be appropriate to women. The jade box was acquired by the Museum as a receptacle for red seal paste, thus making an association with the official world of male bureaucracy and of literate gentlemen, milieus from which women were excluded. In point of fact, the box's decoration is of lychees, a tropical fruit from south China, which carries symbolic meanings concerning fertility and the marriage bed. It could be that incense or a moulded cake of white foundation make-up was kept in this box. Whatever its exact use, the erroneous designation as a seal paste box removed the possibility of a distinctive culture of Chinese women.

The jade is carved with twelve lychee fruits and there are seven different diaper patterns on them. Lattice-work lychees also appear on a sequence of small lacquer boxes, and it is from these more securely datable pieces that the jade box's manufacture is assigned to the years between 1500 and 1580.

The three shallow cups inside the ceramic box on the right in the same picture (60) might have held cosmetics for the face or hair. They are made from glazed stoneware and come from the kilns at Longquan in Zhejiang province. They date from between 1250 and 1350, earlier than the lychee box.

Although there must undoubtedly have been changes in women's make-up over the dynasties, the white foundation plus rouge seem to have formed the basis for face painting for several centuries. The white face preparations were based on rice paste and variously contained lead, aluminium, calcium, silicon, magnesium and silver. The mixture was pressed into differently-shaped moulds which left a floral imprint on the resulting cake of make-up when it was turned out. The chief constituent of Chinese rouge was the flowers of the 'red indigo' plant from Gansu province. The petals were dried in the sun, and then either powdered or infused to make a dye. For application to the face this was mixed with animal fat, giving it the consistency of a cream and so producing a shine rather than a matt finish when used alone. The presence of animal lard must have necessitated its being made in small amounts to be used quickly before it went rancid. Paper leaves coated with rouge were a Qing dynasty improvement, but this method must have given a different effect.

59
LACQUER BOX
1150–1250, Southern Song dynasty
Height 16.4 cm
FE.151-1983
南宋漆盒

TWO SILVER BOXES
675–750, Tang dynasty
Diameters 7, 5.5 cm
M.125-1938, M.34-1935
唐初 — 中期銀盒 (二)

Women of the leisured classes were pampered by a hierarchy of maids, at least one of whom would have had responsibility for applying make-up. The finished results were scrutinised in metal mirrors, the front of these being polished until they shone sufficiently to give a reflection. The smooth surface quickly darkens and relinquishes its reflective qualities and so it is the decorated backs of these

Lady dressing her hair (below)
Illustration to the drama
< 琵琶記 > The Lute (1573–1619)

60 (opposite)
BRONZE MIRROR (back)
Song dynasty (960–1279)
Diameter 17.5 cm
M.78-1937
宋銅鏡

MIRROR STAND (back bottom)
Gilt bronze
1100–1350, Song-Yuan dynasties
Length 27 cm
M.737-1910
宋 — 元金銅鏡座

CERAMIC COSMETIC BOX
(right)
Longquan ware
1250–1350, Song-Yuan dynasties
Diameter 11 cm
C.29-1935
南宋 — 元龍泉窰瓷粉盒

JADE BOX (left)
1500–80, Ming dynasty
Diameter 6.1 cm
FE.154-1988
明中期玉盒

mirrors which today generate most interest; an example is shown here (60). Glass was not much used in making Chinese mirrors before the twentieth century. Although some mirrors do have handles they were more usually held by a cord running through two holes in the central knob on the back. Here, the mirror rests in a gilt-bronze stand in the form of a magic creature, called a *xiniu*, looking round at the moon represented by the mirror above a bank of clouds.

The devotional image (*61*) probably graced a woman's room. Personal images might be from the Buddhist or Daoist pantheons and other religious cults and, for a pious person, their presence was thought to aid the fulfilment of life's great objectives: riches, happiness, long life, promotion in the official hierarchy and numerous sons. The small statue of the Buddhist deity Guanyin holding a baby boy is a touching reminder of the Chinese wife's duty to bear male children. Such figures were talismans personal to women, who prayed to them for an end to infertility and gave thanks to them on the birth of a son.

The figure is made from ivory and was carved between 1580 and 1640. The tusk from which it was made would have been imported into China from Africa, south-east Asia or India, elephants having become rare in China by the Song dynasty (960–1279). On this piece the surface patina of the ivory is partly hidden by red lacquer and gilding. The flowing sleeve ends of Guanyin's gown swing in the same direction as she and the child gaze. It is a graceful and contemplative figure; we can only speculate on the solace it brought.

Recent research favours the view that these statuettes of Guanyin were made in Zhangzhou in the south-eastern coastal province of Fujian. The ivory carvers there had been commissioned by Spanish traders to produce figures of the Virgin and Child of Christianity and they then progressed to making images of the 'son-giving Guanyin' for the domestic market.

Women's lives were arguably more changed by marriage than were men's. A daughter left her parents' home at this time to take up residence with her husband's family. Most conspicuous amongst the goods and chattels travelling along with a bride to her husband's family home was the canopied bed, an unmistakable and potent symbol of the anticipated fertility of the young wife (*52*). The bed remained her personal property and she would take it away with her if the marriage broke down. A wedding in China was a serious contract between two families. The ceremony was preceded by lengthy negotiations usually conducted by a marriage broker, the bride and groom playing no part at this stage. In fact, the couple were unlikely to meet each other before the wedding day when the bride would leave her own family mansion in a closed sedan chair and be taken to the man's home along with her dowry. This would include the bride's trousseau, which she and the other female clan members would often have begun embroidering before any betrothal plans were set in motion.

61

FIGURE OF GUANYIN

Lacquered and gilded ivory
1580–1640, Ming dynasty
Height 32 cm
A.15-1935
明晚期金漆象牙雕觀音

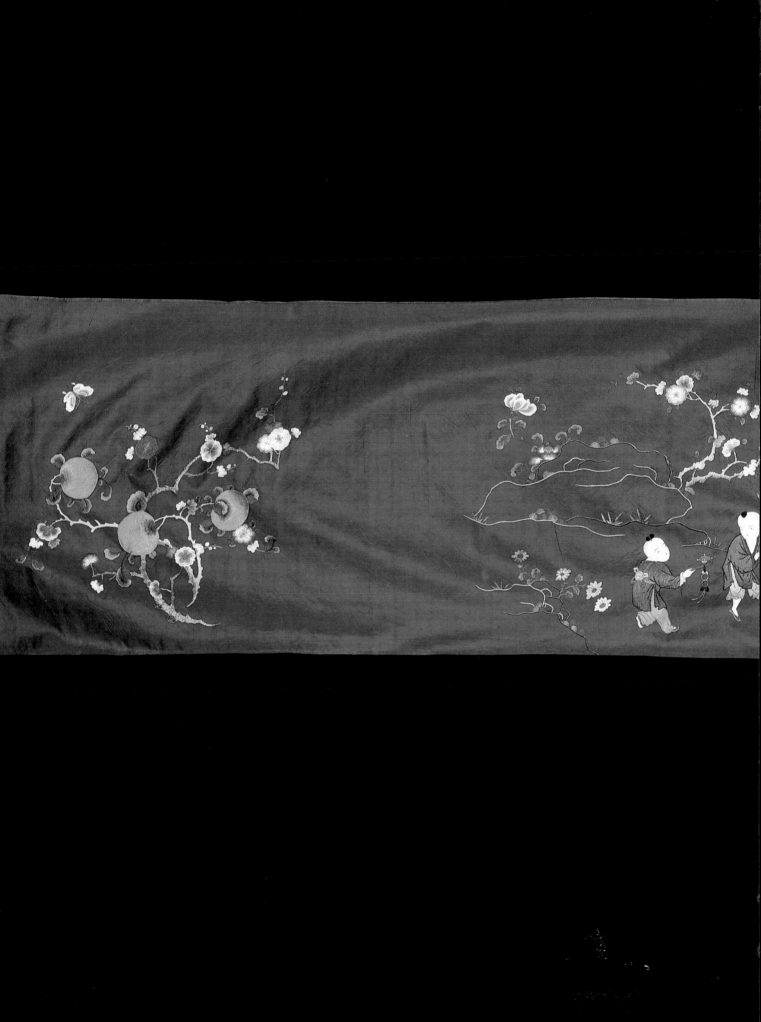

The embroidered wedding hanging, part of which is shown here (62), may have been used as a valance to go around the top of a bed, its theme of boys at play stressing the idea of marriage as a vehicle for ensuring the continuation of the male line. One boy rides down from the clouds mounted on a dragon. He clasps his hands around the beast's horns to steady himself. To one side of him, another boy is in charge of a handsome phoenix bird while four other children look on. The musical instrument held by the boy in the pink coat and green trousers is a *sheng*, a mouth organ of great antiquity in China, and its name in Chinese has the same sound as the word meaning 'to be born'. The infant in the dark blue coat and yellow trousers holds out a sceptre with silk tassels dangling from it. This embodies the idea that everything will go as you wish and the meaning is also derived from a play on words.

The long box (63) is decorated in carved black lacquer on a red ground, a technique strikingly reminiscent of the bold outlines of book illustration, which flourished at the time it was manufactured towards the end of the Ming dynasty. It too shows scenes related to marriages, and was probably used in one of the crucial ceremonies leading up to a wedding, the exchange of horoscopes between the families of the bride and groom. These astrological charts were important to ensure that the couple's destinies were linked together, for if the signs were unfavourable the marriage was unlikely to succeed. The subjects on the box are all stories which have a bearing on marriages. At the top, the mythical Emperor Yao respectfully seeks the horoscope of his son and prospective successor Shun, from Shun's harsh old father, Gu Sou, 'The Blind Elder'. The large central scene shows an aristocratic bride arriving in a decorated carriage at her new home. At the bottom, Li Yuan, future founder of the Tang dynasty, wins Dou Yi's daughter as his bride by triumphing in an archery competition, hitting the eyes of two peacocks painted on a screen. These are stories which have their origins in very formal types of classical literature, but they would have been familiar to a much wider audience through their existence as the subjects of dramas. These dramas would have been performed at weddings, and so the messages they conveyed about parental authority and women's submission would have been inculcated from a very early age, particularly among women, who even in upper-class households were often not able to read. A number of these distinctively shaped and decorated horoscope boxes survive, but they all date from around 1600. This suggests that the customs involving them were particular to the late Ming period.

62 (*previous pages*)
EMBROIDERED HANGING
1800–1900, Qing dynasty
Entire hanging 70 × 523 cm
T.26-1952
Harrison-Topham Gift
清晚期綉綢兒戲圖軸

63 (*right*)
LACQUER BOX
1600–40, Ming dynasty
Length 64.2 cm
983-1883
明晚期雕漆盒

Eating and Drinking

THE Chinese enthusiasm for food can be seen in the specially prepared and presented edibles at celebrations and religious festivals, in the careful combining of certain foods thought to promote good health and long life, and in the abundant restaurants and 'take-aways' serving Chinese dishes in and outside China. Parts of China have known terrible famine years and perhaps the need to make a little go a long way has made Chinese cooks more ingenious with the scant ingredients available. The rich endemic plant and animal life there has been exploited to the full in producing what must be considered as one of the world's greatest cuisines.

The Chinese divide their foodstuffs into two broad categories, *fan* and *cai*. The first consists of grains and starch foods. Rice, millet and wheat are examples of *fan*. *Cai* are vegetables and meat. Each group has its own utensils for cooking and serving, and a balanced meal must contain both *fan* and *cai*. Dairy products and raw foods are not traditionally part of the Chinese diet although preserved food is widely used to prolong seasonal choices and also to protect against food shortages.

Rice is grown and eaten mainly in south China. The cookery of north China is characterised by wheat, millet and sorghum because these are the cereal crops which grow best there. This difference has been evident since Neolithic times (about 5000–about 1700 BC) although more localised regional cookery, such as 'Cantonese' and 'Sichuan', where the meals have distinctive flavours or sets of ingredients, is of more recent date.

Apart from the staples mentioned above, the foodstuffs we most associate with Chinese cookery are pork, chicken, fish, soybean, mushroom, Chinese cabbage, a variety of fruits and the flavourings red pepper, soya sauce, ginger, garlic, and spring onion. Boiling, stir-frying and steaming are the principle methods of cooking, while baked dishes are uncommon.

Some of the culinary practices considered essentially Chinese have their roots in the Zhou dynasty (1050–221 BC) or before. For instance, the distinction between *fan* and *cai* and the art of combining ingredients into a satisfying 'dish' are two customs for which early antecedents can be found. The long documented history of food in China attests to this continuity in certain key areas and archaeology has provided further evidence in the form of eating, drinking and cooking vessels made of bronze, some of which are tellingly inscribed.

The three-legged cauldron (*64*) was used in connection with feasting as were most of the remarkable bronze vessels from China's distant past. Such vessels were subsequently included in burials (see p.36). These variously-shaped bronzes along with a battery of pottery utensils seem to have held specific foodstuffs or drinks. The designs of packed spirals surrounding awesome monster masks which recur on many of the bronzes must have added to the solemnity of the death rituals and ancestor rites for which they were used. It is likely that a tripod such as this one

64
BRONZE TRIPOD, *Li Ding*
About 1225–1100 BC, Shang dynasty
Height 19 cm
M.60-1953
商晚期銅鬲鼎

was used as a cooking pot for grain. Bronze seems to have been reserved for grain foods which, during this early period, consisted principally of several different kinds of millet. The three legs would have straddled a fire conveniently while the handles would have been a help when removing it from the heat. We do not know if each participant ate directly from such a vessel or whether portions were served into individual bowls. It may be that the food was an offering for spirits and not consumed by people at all.

This tripod was made about 3,000 years ago and is called a *li ding*, a composite term coined by antiquarians in the Southern Song dynasty (1128–1279) because it combined features of two other types of bronze container, the lobed *li* and the round *ding*. Each of these ancient vessel types has a name, none of them readily translatable from the Chinese. Some of the names appear on the vessels themselves, some of them have been gleaned from texts compiled in the Han dynasty (206 BC–AD 221) but supposedly referring to earlier times, and some shapes have been named retrospectively by later generations. The powerful appeal of these bronzes is heightened by knowing something about the ways in which they were used by the ruling classes of ancient China. Enjoyment of eating is undisguised even though the texts from which we learn about food are mainly discourses on ritual.

Frugality, practised by peasants as a necessity, and preached at various times by philosophers and statesmen, was not a virtue evident in the lives of the Chinese rich whose belongings have come down to us today. The gold dish from the Song dynasty (65) speaks of a prosperity beyond the reach of all but the very wealthy. Gold would have appeared on dinner tables only at the imperial court or in the homes of the exceedingly rich. The small size of the dish suggests that it was used as a serving dish for sweetmeats or pickles, or for an individual helping, in which case it was likely to have been part of a large service. We cannot know exactly what was served in or eaten from this dish. The lotus design in the centre is unlikely to have any link with the food served in it even though Chinese people consume both lotus roots and seeds.

At the time this dish was made it has been suggested that city dwellers in China were the best fed in the world. Despite a population of 100 million, Song China experienced few famines. Food distribution networks flourished and a greater reliance on rice cultivation, boosted by the introduction of several new strains, meant there was an abundance of that cereal and hence a willingness to grow and use a variety of foodstuffs. Cooking, it has been argued, was transformed into a culinary art at this time.

Although wealthy households employed cooks, it seems that the best cooking was found in restaurants. The chefs were men although the establishments themselves were sometimes owned and managed by women. Eating out was and still is one of the great traditional pastimes among Chinese communities everywhere. From the Ming dynasty (1368–1644), boats on Hangzhou's scenic West Lake were fitted out as floating restaurants and could be hired for a meal.

The table and chair (66) date from the Ming dynasty. By this time, the Chinese élite had adopted the habit of sitting on chairs rather than kneeling on the floor. There is no exact date for what must in any case have been a gradual transition, but some evidence from the years between 900 and 1100 make these two centuries the most crucial in the changeover. The introduction of high tables and chairs literally

65
GOLD DISH
Northern Song dynasty (960–1127)
Diameter 14.6 cm
M.29-1935
北宋金碟

elevated Chinese meals and must have had some effect on food practices, perhaps chiefly, on the way food was served.

Tables might be used for several purposes, but the one here can really lay claim to being a dining table. The edges on all its sides are raised above the general level of the top surface. Translated from the Chinese, this is called the 'water stopping line', and it is designed to prevent spillages falling into the laps of the diners. A table of this square shape would have accomodated several people. The narrow rectangular tables also found in the Chinese interior accomodated only one or at

Banquet scene *(below)*
Illustration to the drama
< 千金記 > *A Thousand Pieces of Gold* (1573–1619)

66 *(opposite)*
DINING TABLE
Huali wood
1550–1600, Ming dynasty
Height 85.7 cm
FE.67-1983
Addis Bequest
明晚期花梨木飯桌

ARMCHAIR
'Chicken wing' wood
1550–1600, Ming dynasty
Height 106 cm
FE.27-1989
明晚期雞翅木扶手椅

(left to right on table)

JADE EWER
1550–1600, Ming dynasty
Height 23 cm
FE.4-1990
明晚期玉壺

PORCELAIN BOX AND LID
Jiajing reign period mark (1522–66),
Ming dynasty
Diameter 19 cm
C.128-1928
Bloxam Gift
明嘉靖瓷盒

JADE STEMCUP
1400–1600, Ming dynasty
Height 10.6 cm
FE.71-1977
明玉高足杯

PORCELAIN BOWL
Wanli reign period mark
(1573–1619), Ming dynasty
Diameter 15.3 cm
C.127-1928
Bloxam Gift
明萬歷瓷碗

most two people so if there were lots of participants for the meal a number of these tables would have to be set out. In upper class households men generally ate separately from women and children. In poorer homes, where the whole family ate together, men were served first. Tablecloths were not used to cover the table top although decorative textile frontals sometimes hung around the sides (see p.116).

The chair shown with the table could have functioned as a dining chair but it may have been used in other contexts as well. The graining on the timber, a species of *Ormosia*, has resulted in its being called 'chicken-wing wood' by the Chinese. Chairs with arms were the preserve of wealthier men and women high up in the family ranking. Other women and the less well-off made do with stools.

The bowl is the vessel shape we most identify with east-Asian eating and drinking. Bowls are used for a variety of foods besides rice and, on the whole, they are made from porcelain. This one (67) is unusual in that it is carved out of rhinoceros horn. Most other surviving bowls of this material are smaller and intricately carved, and would have been for alcohol. Chinese food is chopped into bite-size pieces before being cooked. Chopsticks, which have been in use since Shang times (about 1700–1050 BC), are more appropriate cutlery than knives and forks. The meal comes to the table in serving dishes and the contents are distributed amongst the diners into smaller individual dishes and bowls like this one. The naturally-occurring colour gradations in the raw material have resulted in this rhinoceros horn bowl being dark brown at the base, becoming paler towards the flaring mouth. Both the rim and the solid pedestal foot have a squared scroll running around them. Zhangzhou, a city in south-east China which we have already noted as a centre for ivory carving (see p.144), is a possible site of this bowl's manufacture.

The rhinoceros survived up to the fourteenth century in Yunnan in the far south-west of China, but by the time this bowl was made the horn would have been imported. The belief that rhinoceros horn is an antidote to poison goes back in China to the fourth century BC and it seems likely that peoples of western Asia and the Roman empire adopted this idea from the Chinese.

67
R HINOCEROS HORN BOWL
1550–1640, Ming dynasty
Diameter 15 cm
FE.28-1983
明晚期犀牛角碗

Food was also sent as presents. The more lavish the container in which the edible gifts were presented, the greater was deemed the esteem of the giver. The lacquered wooden box shown here (68), a luxury item from the period 1500–1600, would have marked out the ordinary contents as having special social meaning. The recipient of the present did not keep the box but sent it back with a return gift. The inside of the box is plain without any fittings so that it could accomodate different types of food. Cakes could be separately wrapped and packed, and small savoury items set in saucers or steamers. By contrast, the outside is highly decorated with bands of scrolling running across the vertical grooves which divide the surface of the box into eight segments. The handsome design, known as *jian huan*, 'sword pommel rings', was carved through alternating red and black layers of lacquer giving the piece a pleasing bi-coloured appearance.

68
FOOD BOX
Lacquered wood
1500–1600, Ming dynasty
Diameter 26.4 cm
FE.12-1974
Given by Sir Harry and Lady Garner
明晚期雕漆食盒

Another kind of food container is shown in plate (*69*). The square box has a plain black lacquer base and a red basketwork lid woven from two different thicknesses of bamboo spills. Nine separate dishes fit neatly inside and rest on a removable tray. The fittings are lacquered black and painted with good omen motifs in gold over a red undercoat. This set of dishes is likely to have been taken on picnics or used for meals in the garden. It either held the cold starters which preceded the main meal or else the snacks taken between courses.

Like many other people, the Chinese like to take advantage of fair weather to be outside, and the pleasures of being in a garden or country setting are enhanced by a spread of picnic food. Shen Fu, an endearing but politically unsuccessful civil servant, recounts in his autobiographical sketch *Six Records of a Floating Life* of 1809 how he made an outing with his wife and friends to see the rape flowers in blossom in two of Suzhou's famous gardens. The trip was made all the more enjoyable because they took food and drink with them and sat in the shade of a willow tree for their rustic meal.

Since Neolithic times Chinese people have enjoyed drinking alcoholic beverages as an accompaniment to meals, especially those of a celebratory nature. It is telling that Shen Fu's picnic party was anxious to toast the blossoms in warmed alcohol. It would not have been so appropriate or pleasurable if the drink had been cold. Yun, Shen's wife, ingeniously hired an itinerant dumpling seller to bring along his stove and thus make this possible.

69
SET OF FOOD DISHES
Lacquered wood and split bamboo
1700–40, Qing dynasty
34.7 × 34.7 cm
FE.44-1983
清早期編竹描金漆盒

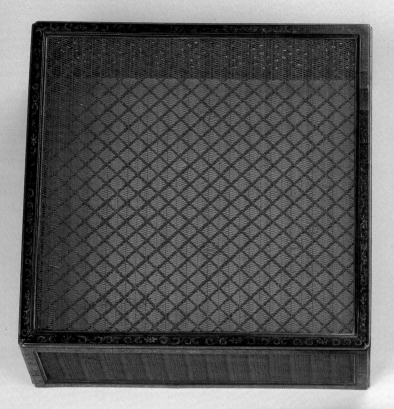

It seems that certain alcoholic drinks have always been drunk warm in China. This ceramic vessel (70), made some time between 500 and 580, was used for heating alcohol. Its small size, just fourteen centimetres high, means that it would have held one or two servings. The hollow handle at one side of the pot would have taken a wooden extension to lift it off the stove and the ceramic loop opposite this could also have accomodated a removable handle to lend extra stability. At the back there is an animal's tail, a seemingly rather frivolous piece of decoration as the vessel does not have an animal face on it.

Wine warmers like this often do have beast-like heads or faces and the tripod legs are usually fashioned into hooves or paws. Bronze vessels of this type have

Scene from the drama ＜雙魚記＞
A Pair of Fish (1573–1619) *(left)*

70 *(right)*
CERAMIC TRIPOD
About 500–580, Six dynasties period
Height 14 cm
C.432-1922
六朝釉瓷壺

been found dating from the Han dynasty (206 BC–AD 220) and some of these are inscribed with the word *jiao* meaning 'to heat', thus partly confirming their use.

Chinese alcoholic drinks are mostly produced from cereal grains and at first they were fermented. Some time after the Tang dynasty (618–906) distilled grain liquors were introduced although fermented beverages continued to be drunk as well. Fruit wines exist in China but they have never played a big part in Chinese drinking habits. An imaginative range of ceramic and metal drinking cups, servers and storage jars were continuously manufactured and the elegance of the tableware enticed customers to wineshops as much as the quality of the alcohol. The services of prostitutes were also part of the allure of certain drinking establishments.

It is possible that alcohol was stored in large lidded jars like those in plates (71) and (72). The earlier of the two may have been made for a grave. Providing refreshments for the spirits of the dead is a continuing practice in Chinese burial customs (see p.38) and ceramics with lead glazes, like the one here, have frequently been found in ancient tombs. There is no evidence to suggest, however, that the Chinese of bygone ages knew about the poisonous properties of lead and it seems possible that lead-glazed objects were not exclusively reserved for the life here-after. The other jar (72) is decorated in underglaze cobalt blue and overglaze iron red with fishes, waving waterweed and lotuses. The watery design serves as a reminder that, with some exceptions, it is not possible to know whether any of the jars shown here are for alcohol or water.

There are no such doubts about the use of the jar in plate (73). The inscription around the shoulder reads 'fine wine with delicate aroma' and this same formula appears on other pieces from the Longquan kilns in Zhejiang province. It may be a trade mark. The contents of the wider-mouthed jars described above would have been ladled out or scooped up, whereas the liquid would be poured from this jar. This makes it a serving vessel as well as a storage jar, the Chinese equivalent of a glass wine bottle. A plug would have been wedged into the mouth and the whole top sealed.

71 (right)
CERAMIC JAR
Liao dynasty (907–1125)
Height 40.7 cm
C.10-1935
遼彩繪瓷罐

72 (overleaf left)
PORCELAIN JAR
Jiajing reign period mark (1522–66),
Ming dynasty
Height 40.6 cm
Circ.118-1936
明嘉靖瓷罐

73 (overleaf right)
PORCELAIN JAR
1350–1400, Yuan-Ming dynasties
Height 47 cm
FE.34-1972
Lee Gift
元 — 明初瓷瓶

Another pouring and storing vessel, almost certainly for alcohol, is shown in plate (74). It is a handsome stoneware jar with bold decoration cut through the black glaze. It dates from the twelfth to thirteenth century and is a type known as Cizhou after one of the major centres of production. Like the inscribed jar above it would have had a stopper.

The jar in plate (75) is in the shape of a leather flask. It was made in north China at a time when a people whose original homeland lay outside the borders of China, the Qidan, ruled in that area as the Liao dynasty (907–1125). Their nomadic existence necessitated transportable pouches made from animal skins secured with gut or rope. Not only has the general shape been translated into ceramic form but the ties have been copied as well. We do not know what the market was for this kind of jar. They could have been made for the Qidan themselves and may signify their changed, less wandering, lifestyle; or Han Chinese consumers may have found the shape a novelty, one that was convenient to lift and from which it was convenient to pour.

The small vessel in plate (76) is an example of an individual pot for alcohol. There would have been one for each guest. Servants would bring round a large pouring vessel and top up the smaller ewers. The yellow one exemplifies the eighteenth-century taste for the antique as it is based on a bronze form called a *he* from the seventh to sixth centuries BC. The ancient *he* was also used for alcohol. The yellow of the glaze, despite being an appropriate colour for imperial use, does not necessarily mean that this pot was used in court circles. It bears no reign mark and like many yellow silk robes it is doubtful whether it has any links at all with the Qing emperors (see p.185).

74 (right)
STONEWARE JAR
Jin dynasty (1115–1234)
Height 27.3 cm
Circ.442-1928
金系耳瓷瓶

75 (overleaf left)
CERAMIC JAR
910–1000, Liao dynasty
Height 21.6 cm
C.103-1913
遼釉瓷皮囊壺

76 (overleaf right)
PORCELAIN POURING VESSEL
1680–1720, Qing dynasty
Height 14 cm
C.502-1910
Salting Bequest
清早期釉瓷壺

Plates (77) to (81) show a selection of drinking vessels from different periods. The goblet of bronze (77) was used around 1150–1050 BC in a Shang dynasty rite. Its size (32 cm high) may indicate that it was passed round from one participant to the next, a communal rather than an individual cup. Equally it may have served as a libation cup to honour ancestors. Precious metal vessels had been used for eating and drinking as early as the late Zhou dynasty, about 400 BC. Gold and silver were not so highly regarded in ancient China as in the West (for example, the civilisations of Rome or Iran) and it was only in the Tang dynasty that they became sought after. In the early Tang period of about 640–700 trade between China and her western neighbours increased, with a large volume of traffic travelling both ways along the Silk Routes. One prized commodity in China was silver imported from Iran, for which demand soon outstripped supply. Chinese silversmiths started work, but as they had no developed industrial tradition, many imported forms and decorations were imitated. That is why some of the shapes of Tang silver, for example that of the cups at the back and right of plate (78), look foreign. Archaeological evidence indicates that silver vessels were used both by the imperial family and by high-ranking officials, and that they were greatly valued. The Tang cups shown here, unlike the earlier bronze goblet (77), were probably not shared, although we cannot be sure about the prevailing etiquette. The flower-shaped silver-gilt cup would not have been an easy shape to drink from, whereas the cup with a handle and the stemcup are certainly for alcohol. The ladle at the front of the picture would probably also have been used in preparations for drinking; a smaller, flatter type of spoon is found at the same period for use with food. During the succeeding Song period the possession of precious metal vessels became more commonplace, although gold and silver were still expensive. The gold cup with a flange above a loop handle in the centre of (78) shows that foreign shapes continued to be copied; pieces of comparable form have been found at a site near the northern branch of the Silk Routes (see map p.18). While we cannot be sure that such cups were invariably used for alcohol, it seems likely that this was the case. The rather unusual agate cup (79) has both practicality and attractiveness on its side.

77 (right)
BRONZE GOBLET
1150–1050 BC, Shang dynasty
Height 32 cm
FE.156-1988
Marchetti Gift
商晚期銅觚

78 (overleaf left)
GOLD CUP *(centre)*
Northern Song dynasty (960–1127)
Diameter 7 cm
M.30-1935
北宋金耳杯

THREE SILVER CUPS
Tang dynasty (618–906)
Maximum height 5.1 cm
M.31, 32, 33-1935
唐銀杯（三）

SILVER LADLE
Tang dynasty (618–906)
Length 19.4 cm
M.101-1938
唐銀勺

79 (overleaf right)
AGATE CUP
1100–1200, Song dynasty
Diameter 10.1 cm
C.1850-1910
Salting Bequest
宋雕瑪瑙杯

Stemcups were only for alcohol, never for tea (*80*). They are called *quan bei* in Chinese, which can be translated as 'toasting cups' or more literally as 'urging cups', the implication being that the drinker toasts his companions and at the same time urges them to quaff another cup. Chinese manners dictate that each member of the assembled company proclaims his lack of interest in drinking, but in reality a great deal of imbibing goes on. Perhaps this studied indifference accounts for there being no word for 'hangover' in the Chinese language. Of the three stemcups shown here, one is of jade and two are of porcelain (*80*). Recent excavations carried out at the imperial kiln sites at the 'porcelain city' of Jingdezhen reveal that both the porcelain cups were made for the Ming court during the reign of the Emperor Yongle (1403–24). The red glazed example is extremely rare, dating as it does to the early Yongle period, although the Museum has a second such cup in its collections. The excavations at Jingdezhen reveal also that there was a huge wastage of the red glazed pieces with eighty percent of those made not coming up to standard.

80

PORCELAIN STEMCUP
WITH RED GLAZE (*left*)
Yongle reign period (1403–24),
Ming dynasty
Height 10.5 cm
C.168-1905
Gulland Gift
明永樂紅釉瓷高足杯

JADE STEMCUP (*centre*)
1400–1600, Ming dynasty
Height 10.9 cm
FE.71-1977
明玉高足杯

WHITE PORCELAIN
STEMCUP (*right*)
Yongle reign period mark (1403–24),
Ming dynasty
Height 10.4 cm
C.30-1953
明永樂白釉瓷高足杯

Scene from the prose collection
< 狀元圖考 > *Illustrated Study of
Examination Successes* (1573–
1619) *(left)*

81 *(right)*
JADE CUP
1550–1640, Ming dynasty
Length 19.5 cm
1552-1882
Wells Bequest
明晚期雕玉杯

A different shaped cup *(81)*, dating from the period 1550–1640, would seem less easy to drink from than the stemcups, but in fact the ornate pierced carving provides two handles and there is a gap in the decoration just big enough to fit the mouth. There are some references to tea being drunk from jade cups in the Ming dynasty but this particular type would seem to be a standard alcohol cup. The design of cranes would have been regarded by some Ming arbiters of taste as rather vulgar.

Tea is China's most common beverage and China is the world's largest tea-producing nation. The tea bush, related to the camellia, grew wild there and the Chinese were the first people to cultivate it for culinary and medical use. Tea is served as an accompaniment to meals and snacks and is also taken on its own throughout the day. Chinese people prefer green unfermented tea which is drunk hot without milk or sugar.

Different kinds of utensils have been used to make and serve tea because methods of preparation have changed over the centuries. When tea drinking first started in south China in the Han dynasty, it was made like a soup. At other times the tea was formed into cakes and pieces were either broken off and thrown into boiling water or else the cake was ground into a powder. The influential *Classic of Tea* by the eighth-century tea master, Lu Yu, promoted tea drinking to an aesthetic experience among the leisured and well-to-do. He advocated that they use green glazed tea bowls because this improved the depth of the tea's green colour.

The popularity of green bowls waned and black stoneware bowls, like the one on the stand illustrated here (*82*) which was made in north China, were particularly prized during the Song period. Bowls with dark glazes were made in several different areas and were used locally. The most famous type, however, was black ware from the Jian kilns in Fujian province. This was because Fujian also grew excellent quality tea, which found favour at court. Thus Jian ware tea bowls were transported north along with the Fujian tea. Some of the bowls even bear the mark of tribute pieces destined for the palace in the Northern Song capital, Kaifeng, in present-day Henan province.

By this time in China, tea drinking was an everyday habit for all levels of society and in certain circles it was considered an art. Aristocrats, rich gentlemen and educated monks and nuns gathered together to appreciate fine teas and tea utensils. They held elegant tea contests which, like many of the black bowls and the good tea, originated in Fujian. Tea powder and hot water were whisked up into a froth and the competitor whose froth lasted longest was declared the winner. This tea with its white whipped topping showed up well against black ceramic bowls.

Although the black bowls continued to be manufactured, imperial patronage came to an end with the Southern Song dynasty (1128–1279). They continued, however, to be appreciated in Japan where they were known as 'temmoku' and exerted a powerful influence on the native ceramic industry.

Stoneware bowls do not lose heat through their thick sides as quickly as porcelain ones. This means that the tea stays hot longer and the bowl is less likely to scald the tea drinker's fingers. Stands for bowls extend this idea. As the bowls have no handles, the steaming tea is more easily passed to a guest on a stand which perhaps can be best described as something between a tray and a saucer. The stand shown here, on the left, is made from lacquered wood although ceramic ones also occur. The inscription on it records that it was made in what is today Changsha, the capital city of Hunan province, and includes a cyclical date corresponding to 1034 or 1094.

The modern tea bowl, on the right, in the same picture, was made in 1984 as a conscious imitation of earlier pieces. It came from the kilns at Zibo in Shandong province where dark-bodied wares with brown glazes derived from iron have been made since the Song dynasty. The random spotting on both bowls in the picture,

82

STONEWARE TEA
BOWL (*top left*)
1100–1200, Song-Jin dynasties
Diameter 10.2 cm
C.18-1935
宋 — 金瓷茶碗

STAND FOR A BOWL
(*bottom left*)
Lacquered wood
Dated 1034 or 1094, Song dynasty
Height 6.2 cm
W.3-1938
北宋漆碗托

STONEWARE TEA BOWL
(*right*)
Zibo kilns, Shandong province
1984
Diameter 11.9 cm
FE.51-1984
現代山東淄博窰瓷茶碗

an effect called 'oil spot', is done purposefully and is caused by iron in the glaze rising to the surface during firing. In recent times, tea bowls similar to this were available to the general public through department stores near the kiln site at a modest price. The poor distribution networks within China, however, meant that such items were never available to people living outside the vicinity of their manufacture. It is believed that the factory has now ceased making products of this type.

By contrast, the Yixing kilns in Jiangsu province provide one of the few areas in modern Chinese craft production to have maintained and even improved standards. These kilns have been famous for their teapots ever since the sixteenth century, by which time leaf tea had replaced powdered tea and teapots came into use to brew the dried and rolled tea leaves. These two teapots (*83*) were produced at Yixing; the one on the left during the decade 1650–60, the one on the right in 1984.

Today, thirteen thousand people work in the ceramic industry in Yixing but only a small proportion of them are engaged in making the distinctive stoneware teapots. The local clays have a high sand content and can be cream, red, or a warm brown, the colour of the examples shown. The teapots are not usually glazed but are burnished and fired. Production line examples can be obtained reasonably cheaply but those made by named potters are prized by collectors and command high prices. The fact that the potters sign their pieces makes them exceptional among China's largely anonymous craft. Another factor which endears Yixing teapots to tea drinkers is their total suitability for tea making. They keep the tea warm, pour well, and their small size reduces wastage of good leaves.

The teapot on the left was made by the potter, Hui Mengchen whose ideal small pear-shaped teapots strongly influenced later craft workers. This one is thought to be a precursor of that famous shape. The woman potter, Jiang Rong (born 1919), made the teapot on the right, and she is now honoured in China as a National Craft Master having started potting at the age of eleven under the guidance of her father. Her fame and skill mean that pieces like this water chestnut teapot are rarely used to brew tea, although the pot made by Hui Mengchen, no less famous a potter, has some signs of sediment inside.

83
TEAPOT (*left*)
Yixing kilns, Hui Mengchen
1650–60, Qing dynasty
Height 8.3 cm
C.871-1936
清初惠孟臣造宜興窰茶壺

TEAPOT (*right*)
Yixing kilns, Jiang Rong
1984
Height 5.8 cm
FE.31-1984
現代江榮設計宜興窰茶壺

Ruling

FROM the earliest times, the rulers of China have been able to call on makers in a large number of crafts to produce particularly fine objects which added to their prestige. The bronze vessels of the first historic dynasties are the earliest surviving testimony to this. By the Ming (1368–1644) and Qing (1644–1911) dynasties a variety of workshops existed in the immediate vicinity of the 'Forbidden City', the huge imperial palace set in the very centre of Peking, to supply luxury items for court use and for the emperors to give as marks of their favour. Very large collections of earlier Chinese art were also built up, particularly in the eighteenth century. Some of these treasures were stolen or sold off in the aftermath of the Republican revolution of 1911, though most of them remain in the collections of the Palace Museum in Peking and the National Palace Museum in Taipei. The prestige of the imperial name, and the added value which it can bring to an object in the market-place, means that any connection with the imperial court and its workshops claimed for an object which is now outside China has to be scrutinised very carefully. Nevertheless, the Victoria and Albert Museum does contain a number of pieces which either certainly or probably emanate from the imperial collections of the Ming and Qing periods. It is therefore on these periods that the following chapter concentrates.

One of the most renowned of all palace workshops was the 'Orchard Factory', which was, according to a number of later sources, set up in the new capital, Peking, at the beginning of the Ming dynasty to produce the finest carved lacquer. A magnificent folding armchair (*84*), decorated with five-clawed dragons writhing among clouds, may well be a product of this workshop, which was situated just to the north-west of the palace compound. Together with a famous and unique table in the same technique, this chair is one of the Museum's most important Chinese treasures. The evidence of paintings shows that such folding chairs were used by the Ming emperors on their travels. Such journeys became less and less frequent as the dynasty progressed, eventually being reduced to brief ceremonial visits to the imperial tombs, set in a valley just over a day's journey from the Forbidden City. The chair carries the mark of the Xuande reign period (1426–35), although stylistically it would appear to date from rather later, towards the middle of the sixteenth century. By at least 1600, such items from the imperial household were being smuggled out of the palace and sold to collectors, at a notorious market held by the north gate of the Forbidden City.

Like their Ming predecessors, the emperors of the Qing dynasty (members of the Manchu ethnic minority from the north-east of China) did not have one single symbol, such as a throne or a crown, which embodied their rule. There was no 'Throne of China' in a literal sense, but rather a number of thrones placed throughout their numerous huge palaces. These were related in style to the couches used by wealthy people generally, but might have decoration particularly suited to the

84
FOLDING ARMCHAIR
Carved lacquer on wood
1500–1560, Ming dynasty
Height 114.5 cm
FE.8-1976
Given by Sir Harry and Lady Garner
明初雕漆交椅

imperial status, as here (85) with five-clawed dragons and exotic figures meant to represent the bearers of tribute from foreign lands. The elephant bearing a vase on its back is a rebus, or visual pun, of a kind which was very popular in the eighteenth century. It carries the hidden meaning 'auguries of great peace', a suitably imperial image. This throne, shown here without any of the cushions which would originally have padded its hard surface, is decorated in layered, carved lacquer of five different colours. It was taken by Russian soldiers in 1900 from one of the imperial 'Travelling Palaces' in the Southern Park, a large area ten kilometres south of Peking used by the Qing emperors for troop reviews, and also for occasional hunting. The largest of the four palaces in the park was extensively

Peking in the Qing dynasty *(left)*
From < 宸垣識略 > *Brief Account of the Imperial Domain* (1788)

85 *(right)*
IMPERIAL THRONE
Carved lacquer on wood
1775–80, Qing dynasty
Height 118 cm, width 125 cm,
depth 92 cm
W.399-1922
Swift Gift
清中期雕漆皇帝寶座

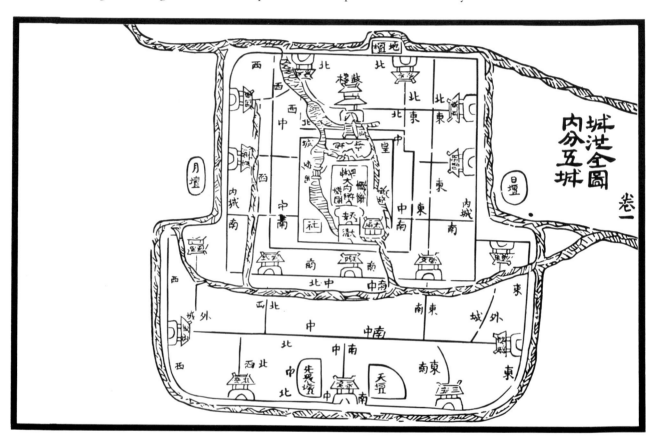

refurbished in 1777, and the style of this throne suggests that it may have been made around that time. As was usual, it was made with a matching screen, which was removed from Peking at the same time and is now in the Museum of Ethnography in Vienna.

The Manchu conquerors who founded the Qing dynasty imposed their own dress and hairstyles on the Chinese population. Particular types of dress were reserved for members of the imperial family, and a particular shade of yellow was used for some, but by no means all, of the robes they wore. Decorative motifs too, and in particular an ancient and enigmatic group of twelve symbols, may mean that a robe was made to be worn by a member of the imperial extended family. Many more imperial robes were made, however, than were ever worn, and lengths of silk from the imperial weaving establishments in the cities of south China were stored away, and were made up into garments and sold after the fall of the empire in 1911. The button fastenings on these rather carelessly tailored garments (86, 87)

86 *(overleaf left)*
DRAGON ROBE FOR AN EMPEROR
Embroidered silk
1800–50, Qing dynasty
142.9 × 193 cm
T.197-1948
清晚期皇帝緞繡龍袍

87 *(overleaf right)*
DRAGON ROBE FOR A WOMAN OF THE IMPERIAL FAMILY
Silk embroidery with coral and pearls
1800–1911, Qing dynasty
144.7 × 199.5 cm
T.253-1967
清晚期嵌珊瑚緞繡女龍袍

seem much too ordinary for the robes of an emperor, and in fact are far inferior to the types of decorated fastenings seen on robes which have remained in the former imperial collections. Hence it is hard to say whether these garments were ever worn by an emperor or member of his immediate family.

The Qing emperors, like all their imperial predecessors, were themselves the chief celebrants of rituals to worship the cosmic powers of Heaven, Earth, the Sun and the Moon. Indeed, in his role as Son of Heaven, only the emperor could perform these rituals, which were believed to be crucial to the continued well-being of the empire and the whole world. This group (88) of glazed porcelain ritual vessels includes one for each of the four altars to these powers, which were situated around the Forbidden City at the four points of the compass. The forms of the vessels were based on some found in the *Illustrated Explanation to the Ritual Implements of the Imperial Dynasty* of about 1760; these models were believed to be bronze

vessels used in rituals at the very dawn of Chinese history. Groups of variously-shaped vessels were made for all four altars; only the colours were different.

The largest and most elaborate of the altars was the Altar of Heaven in the south of Peking. From it comes the deep blue vessel in the form known as *fu*, used for holding food offerings. The lower half dates from the Qianlong reign (1736–95), while the upper half has the mark of the following Jiaqing reign (1796–1820). By the Jiaqing reign, at least seven of these vessels would have been in use at any one time, and it was therefore possible for the parts to have been mixed up in storage. This was even more likely to have happened in the case of the *dou*, of which a yellow example from the Altar of Earth in north Peking is shown. It too dates from the Jiaqing reign, by which time eighty-four of them, filled with a variety of meat, vegetable or pickled dishes would have been in use. The red *zun* from the Altar of the Sun in the east of the city, and its pale blue companion from the western Altar of the Moon, were used for receiving libations of wine, poured from vessels in the *jue* form. Both the *zun* date from the Qianlong reign.

The immense area of the Forbidden City required great quantities of luxury furnishings, such as this display cabinet (89), of painted and carved lacquer on

Ritual vessel, *dou* (*below*)
From a manuscript copy of
< 皇朝禮器圖式 > *Illustrated Explanation to the Ritual Implements of the Imperial Dynasty* (after 1766)

88 (*opposite*)
PORCELAIN VESSELS FROM THE IMPERIAL ALTARS
Yellow *dou* from the Temple of the Earth (*centre top*)
Jiaqing reign period mark (1796–1820), Qing dynasty
Height 29.2 cm
C.17-1968
朝廷祭祀瓷器：
清嘉慶地壇黃釉瓷豆

Red *zun* from the Temple of the Sun (*right*)
Qianlong reign period mark (1736–95), Qing dynasty
Height 27 cm
C.483-1910
Salting Bequest
清乾隆日壇紅釉瓷尊

Dark blue *fu* from the Temple of Heaven (*centre bottom*)
Lower half with Qianlong reign period mark
Upper half with Jiaqing reign period mark
Height 23 cm
FE.99, 100-1970
清乾隆天壇藍釉瓷食器（簠），
嘉慶蓋

Pale blue *zun* from the Temple of the Moon (*left*)
Qianlong reign period mark (1736–95)
Height 27.3 cm
C.526-1910
Salting Bequest
清乾隆月壇藍釉瓷尊

先農壇豆圖

89

a DISPLAY CABINET

Carved and painted lacquer on wood
1720–80, Qing dynasty
Height 105 cm
FE.56-1983
Given by the Museums and Galleries
Commission from the estate of the
late Mrs L. F. Palmer
清中期繪雕漆多寶格

*(shown on it, from left to right,
top to bottom)*
（櫃上展物左至右，上至下）

b JADE HINGE

Qianlong reign period (1736–95),
after 1749
Height 8.3 cm
C.1936-1910
Salting Bequest
乾隆玉鉸連

c PORCELAIN JAR

1725–50
Height 9.8 cm
FE.124-1975
Bushell Gift
清初瓷瓶

d TURKISH JADE JAR

Dated 1770
Height 11.5 cm
C.1815-1910
Salting Bequest
乾隆土兒其玉瓶

e MOULDED GOURD POT

Kangxi reign period mark
(1662–1722)
Height 8.4 cm
FE.21-1986
康熙葫蘆瓶

f PORCELAIN VESSEL
IMITATING BRONZE

Qianlong reign period (1736–95),
after 1749
Height 10.8 cm
C.497-1910
Salting Bequest
乾隆仿銅瓷杯

g ENAMELLED COPPER
CUP AND SAUCER

1730–45
Diameter of saucer 14.6 cm
C.39-1962
雍正琺瑯紅銅碟杯

h ENAMELLED PORCELAIN
BOWL

Yongzheng reign period mark
(1723–35)
Diameter 9 cm
644-1907
雍正琺瑯彩瓷碗

i PORCELAIN VASE

Yongzheng reign period mark
(1723–35)
Height 20 cm
FE.9-1976
Given by Sir Harry and Lady Garner
雍正瓷瓶

j CLOISONNÉ ENAMEL
MUG

Qianlong reign period mark
(1736–95)
Height 9.2 cm
M.776-1910
Salting Bequest
乾隆招絲琺瑯杯

k JADE VASE

Qianlong reign period (1736–95),
after 1749
Height 24.5 cm
C.1948-1910
乾隆玉瓶

l VASE IMITATING GUAN
WARE

Yongzheng reign period mark
(1723–35)
Height 20.7 cm
1846-1888
Watters Gift
雍正仿官窰瓷瓶

m ENAMELLED
PORCELAIN BOWL

Yongzheng reign period mark
(1723–35)
Diameter 22.9 cm
628-1907
Gulland Gift
雍正琺瑯彩瓷碗

n ROCK CRYSTAL VASE

Qianlong reign period (1736–95)
C.1139-1917
Aston Bequest
乾隆水晶瓶

wood. Its origin in the workshops of the Imperial Household Department is confirmed by the use, in the door panel designs, of subjects which appear with identical treatment on objects remaining in the palace collections in China. The interior surfaces are decorated in painted gold lacquer on a highly finished black ground, imitating Japanese lacquer. Jesuit sources reveal the extent to which the lacquer workers of the imperial workshops were able to imitate the fashionable Japanese *maki-e* ('sprinkled picture') lacquers, which were imported to China through Canton and other ports. Canton became the centre for the production of this 'foreign lacquer', partly to satisfy the European demand; we know that workers in this style were commanded to come to Peking to produce pieces, such as this cabinet, for the court. The cabinet is shown here displaying a variety of the type of small decorative items (not all of which have proven imperial connections) for which it was designed. These all date from the eighteenth century, and exemplify several of the main design trends in court art. There is the love of the antique, and of sheer technical ingenuity, as in the ceramic drinking vessel in the shape of an ox's head, which copies an antique bronze down to the typical speckled patina. There is the delight in exotic imports, like the small white jade pot, now known to be of Turkish manufacture, but classed generally at the time as a 'Hindustan jade'. Like many imperial treasures of the time, this piece was inscribed with a poem, dated 1770, composed by the Qianlong emperor himself. This has been translated thus:

> A winding lotus stem supports one luscious bloom,
> From either side spring buds for hands to grasp.
> Carved in the West, 'tis shaped yet like an antique pot,
> Though fashioned not in Eastern Zhou, snake-forms there are;
> Close-textured, roundly-carved the gem-like stamens,
> Whose hair-like lines stand forth from the precious flower.
> Such treasures rare, though leg-less, yet contrive to reach us here.
> O, white colt in an empty valley, I fear lest you flee afar.

Giving of presents formed an important part of the personnel management policies of Ming and Qing emperors. A pair of fans (*90*), painted on paper and with guards and sticks of *zitan* wood, is typical of the type of small scale gift given by the Qing emperors to favoured aristocrats and high officials. The painting is by the court artist, Jiao Bingzhen (active about 1689–1726), who was also valued as a mathematician, and who is known to have collaborated with the Italian Jesuit artist, Giuseppe Castiglione (1688–1768). Jiao Bingzhen acquired from Castiglione some knowledge of western conventions of perspective, of which there are traces in these otherwise traditional landscapes. The calligraphy on the reverse side (not shown) is by Fang Guancheng (1698–1768), who held a number of important administrative offices throughout the eighteenth century. Fang was in Peking at the start of his career in 1721, and again in 1723–25, when the fans were probably produced. There are inscriptions on the guards by two more important Qing officials of the eighteenth and nineteenth centuries, and the fans eventually came into the possession of Li Hongzhang (1823–1901), the leading late Qing statesman and diplomat.

In addition to the products of artists and workshops situated within the Forbidden City itself, the Qing emperors were able to call on the services of workshops in other parts of the empire. Textiles, for example, were not woven inside the

90
PAIR OF FOLDING FANS
Colours on paper, *zitan* wood guards
Painted by Jiao Bingzhen
(active 1689–1726)
Calligraphy by Fang Guancheng
(1698–1768)
1721–25, Qing dynasty
Length (each) 31.7 cm
T.20-1936
Tweedie Gift
清初焦秉眞畫方觀承題折扇（二）

palace. The Qianlong emperor was known to have believed that the finest jade carving was produced in the cities of Suzhou and Yangzhou, in the prosperous lower Yangtze delta area. The palace jade workshops were extended in 1745, though still containing not more than a few dozen workers. Many particularly important commissions were sent to the south, especially after the increased supply of jade stone which followed the conquest, beginning in 1760, of the area of central Asia where it was mined and collected from riverbeds. By 1769 there were nearly a hundred jade craftsmen working within the palace. A *tour de force* of intricate work, certainly from a workshop under imperial patronage, is this carving (*91*) of eight geese, some preening themselves, some about to take flight, among sinuous waterweeds. The carving is naturalistic and detailed, and the whole thing is divided horizontally into two halves, so that the body of each goose forms a small box. It is claimed, though without any firm proof, to have come from the collection of Yixin (1833–98), the first Prince Gong. He was a grandson of the Qianlong emperor, and played a prominent role in attempts to modernise the empire in the nineteenth century. He had many foreign contacts, and the set of boxes may have been a present from him to one of them.

91
JADE BOX IN THE SHAPE OF EIGHT GEESE
1750–1820, Qing dynasty
Diameter 36.2 cm
FE.57-1983
Given by the Museums and Galleries Commission from the estate of the late Mrs L. F. Palmer
清中期玉雕八鵝盒

Another type of object which had to be ordered for the court from a distant part of the empire was porcelain. This was the *guan yao*, 'official ware', of the kilns at Jingdezhen in Jiangxi province. In the eighteenth century in particular, under the direction of a series of talented and energetic supervisors of porcelain production, these ceramics reached new heights of technical control, range of inventiveness and aesthetic quality. They have remained particularly valued in the eyes of Chinese and western collectors to this day. The large dish on the left (*92*) is decorated in overglaze enamels with a scene of a bird on a branch, in a style which originated in court painting of the Song period (960–1279), but which spread throughout all the crafts in the centuries which followed. It bears the mark on the reverse 'made in the Kangxi reign of the Great Qing dynasty', referring to the title of the emperor whose long reign, from 1662 to 1722, made him a close contemporary of Louis XIV of France. The decorative border of the plate is inscribed 'ten thousand years of long life without end', a salutation which has clear echoes of the emperor's familiar title of 'lord of ten thousand years'. A tradition among western and Chinese collectors at the close of the nineteenth century held that this plate, like similar examples which survive in a number of other collections, was made for the sixtieth birthday of the Kangxi emperor in 1713. Sixty years, the completion of a full calendar cycle, is a particularly important birthday in China, and the celebrations on this occasion were lavish and prolonged. Unfortunately, no evidence has yet come to light to support this tradition, and the most we can say is that the plates were made late in the Kangxi reign, probably for some birthday within the extended imperial family.

The small enamelled porcelain bowl, on the right, proclaims its imperial patronage directly, with the mark 'made by imperial command in the Yongzheng reign' (1723–35). The brief reign of the Kangxi emperor's son saw porcelain techniques raised to new heights. In particular, the use of enamels was greatly extended, influenced perhaps by the successes of the imperial workshops in Peking with the technique of enamelling on copper. The imperial workshops were aided in this by European missionaries attached to the court, who were valued more for their technical expertise in the skills of the 'Western Ocean' than for their spiritual message. It is possible that the enamels used on this florid little bowl were prepared in Peking, and then despatched to the kilns at Jingdezhen. The decoration is typical of this group of court ceramics, being densely packed with areas left undecorated. This style can be viewed as something which appeared first on pieces made to imperial commission, but which soon spread throughout the applied arts of China to become extremely common, not least on the humble domestic ceramics employed in Chinese restaurants around the world.

92
DISH
Porcelain decorated over the glaze
1710–22, Qing dynasty
Diameter 25.5 cm
C.3-1947
清初釉上彩瓷碟

BOWL
Porcelain decorated over the glaze
Yongzheng reign period mark
(1723–35), Qing dynasty
Diameter 9 cm
644-1907
清雍正釉上彩瓷碗

The fascination with the ancient past which runs through the court crafts of the eighteenth century is seen on a large porcelain vase (93), also from the Yongzheng reign. Decorated in underglaze blue, it attempts to combine two distinct traditions from ceramic history. The form is that of a stoneware ewer of the seventh century (95, *second from right*), examples of which were in the imperial collection of antiquities. The technique and the style of the decoration refer to the early Ming dynasty, in particular to the first thirty years of the fifteenth century. The hybrid object which results thus brings to mind two powerful and successful ruling houses, the Tang (618–906) and the Ming. They had been founded by emperors of the Han majority population, and in laying claim to their cultural heritage the Manchu rulers were buttressing their claim to possess the Mandate of Heaven, as truly legitimate Sons of Heaven.

93
VASE
Porcelain decorated with underglaze cobalt blue
Yongzheng reign period mark (1723–35), Qing dynasty
Height 52 cm
C.286-1910
清雍正青花瓷瓶

These claims were developed even further in the cultural policies of the Qian-long emperor, at whose order huge projects were instigated to collate and record all past knowledge on every conceivable subject. The imperial library attempted to catalogue every book worth preserving. A vast catalogue of the imperial collection of paintings and calligraphy, which by now contained a high proportion of all the artistic achievements of past dynasties, was prepared. In the field of antiquities, a huge illustrated catalogue of all the bronze vessels held by the court was compiled in 1749, known as the *Imperially Ordained Mirror of Antiquities Prepared in the Xiqing Hall*. Some of the vessels listed in it can still be identified in surviving collections throughout the world. This illustrated book was also used by craftsmen in the imperial workshops as a sourcebook of patterns, forms and decorations for their

唐犧形表座

own work. One such piece is a figure of a sacrificial ox in enamelled and gilt bronze (*94*), with the mark 'done in imitation of the antique in the Qianlong period'. It is a close copy of a figure illustrated in chapter 38 of the *Mirror of Antiquities*, which is described there (probably correctly) as being a stand for some wooden structure, possibly a musical instrument, and as dating (probably wrongly) from the Tang dynasty. The style of the original piece suggests a much earlier date. The enamelling was carried out in two different techniques; the bulk of the green surface is in champlevé technique, where the underlying bronze is chiselled away and the enamel poured into it, while the detailing is in cloisonné technique, where wires soldered onto the surface serve to outline the colours. The visual effect is that of an archaic bronze, turned green through corrosion, which is inlaid in gold. Another object in the collection based on the same printed source is a tiny jade hinge, shown on the top left of the display cabinet (*89*).

As well as amassing contemporary objects in an antiquarian or archaistic style, the Qing emperors were avid collectors of genuine antiquities. The kinds of antique object favoured by court taste are known from the surviving examples in

'Tang dynasty stand in the form of a sacrificial ox' (*left*)
From < 欽定西清古鑒 > *Imperially Ordained Mirror of Antiquities Prepared in the Xiqing Hall* (1749)

94 (*right*)
OX-SHAPED VESSEL
Enamels and gilding on copper
Qianlong reign period (1736–95),
after 1749
Height 19 cm
M.75-1953
清乾隆金琺瑯彩紅銅尊

95
TABLE

Huali and *hongmu* woods
1720–80, Qing dynasty
Length 140.5 cm
FE.76-1983
Addis Bequest
清初 — 中期花梨，紅木桌

(left to right)
（左至右）

BRONZE VESSEL, *Ding*

1100–1000 BC, Shang-Zhou dynasties
Height 20.7 cm
M.2696-1931
商末 — 周初銅鼎

LID OF A VESSEL

Bronze, inlaid with gold and
malachite
206 BC–AD 8, Han dynasty
Height 6.4 cm
M.724-1910
Salting Bequest
西漢錯金嵌孔雀石銅蓋

BOX

Carved lacquer on wood
Yongle reign period mark (1403–24),
Ming dynasty
Diameter 27 cm
W.21-1969
明永樂雕漆盒

BRONZE VASE, *Bian Hu*

206 BC–AD 8, Han dynasty
Height 30.5 cm
M.1161-1926
西漢銅扁壺

CERAMIC VASE

600–700, Sui-Tang dynasties
Height 41.2 cm
C.70-1910
隋 — 唐瓷瓶

JADE CYLINDER, *Cong*

2800–1900 BC, Neolithic
Height 20.6 cm
A.51-1936
新石器時代玉琮

Peking and Taiwan, and from paintings which show the emperor or the court engaged in the delights of connoisseurship. This eighteenth-century table (95), quite possibly from the palace furniture workshop, is itself carved with motifs taken from ancient jades and bronzes. On it are a selection of the types of object in which the palace collections were so rich (though again these specific examples are not claimed as having a proven imperial connection). Their broad chronological range embodies the kinship which a ruler like Qianlong felt with all the most splendid eras of China's past: the bronze vessels of remote antiquity and of the Han dynasty, the ceramics of the Tang and the carved lacquers from the early Ming 'Orchard Factory' workshop.

Some of the most treasured antiques in the imperial collection were examples of the ceramics made for another, much earlier court, that of the emperors of the Song dynasty. Rarest of all ceramic types is *ru* ware, named after the site of the kiln where it was made in Henan province, not far from the Northern Song imperial capital of Kaifeng. This type of blue-grey glazed stoneware, with a slight deliberate crackling all over, was made for no more than four decades prior to the fall of Kaifeng to the non-Han Chinese Jin dynasty in 1127. The court was then transferred south to what is now the city of Hangzhou. The *ru* ware stand for a bowl in the centre of (96) is thus one of the V&A's greatest treasures, its imperial connections made even more secure by the palace name 'Hall of Perfect Old Age' cut neatly into the body. This name is seen on other pieces in the Palace Collections, and is believed to be that of a hall within the Northern Song imperial palace, so named by the aesthete, Emperor Huizong (reigned 1101–27). The stand is shown here along with a piece of *guan* ('official') ware, on the right, the crackled stoneware produced in the vicinity of Hangzhou to the order of the Southern Song court from the middle of the twelfth century. These imperial commissions from an era of great cultural achievement were valued by later rulers, as well as by less exalted collectors. The third piece on the left of the illustration, a vase, was made as a close imitation of *guan* ware in the eighteenth century, demonstrating the court appetite for such products. It did not come from Hangzhou but from the imperial kilns at Jingdezhen and is clearly marked with the reign name of the Emperor Yongzheng. Thus it is not a 'fake' but rather an article reproduced in homage of earlier styles.

96
VASE (*left*)
Porcelain with crackled white glaze
Yongzheng reign period mark
(1723–26), Qing dynasty
Height 20.7 cm
1846-1888
Watters Gift
清雍正開片釉瓷瓶

STAND FOR A WINE CUP
(*centre*)
Ru ware
1090–1127, Northern Song dynasty
Diameter 16.5 cm
FE.1-1970
Given by Sir Harry and Lady Garner
北宋汝窯瓷杯托

VASE (*right*)
Guan ware
1150–1279, Southern Song dynasty
Height 9.9 cm
C.25-1935
南宋官窯瓷瓶

The Qing empire incorporated all of what is now Mongolia and Tibet, and patronage of the Buddhist faith of these regions was an important part of state policy. The particular iconography of the forms of Buddhism practised in these regions, which is often known in English as 'lamaism', deeply affected court art. Yet another product of the court lacquer workshops which shows this clearly is a box (97) decorated with five-clawed dragons and Buddhist deities. The box is now empty but was probably made to contain a spirit tablet (see p.38), bearing the name of a real deceased person or minor deity, which was intended to act as a focus for worship. The superbly intricate carving of the Buddhas Sakyamuni, Maitreya and Amitabha, the Eight Manifestations of the Bodhisattva Guanyin, and an assembly of Bodhisattvas, Heavenly Kings and Luohans, fix the object firmly in a Buddhist context, and it thus cannot have been used in the ancestral cult of the imperial family. The inscription reads 'reverently made in the Qianlong period of the great Qing' and the box may have formed part of a set, at least one identical example being known.

This large hanging (98) is embroidered with a *mandala*, a mystic diagram of the Womb Treasury World, the universal source, matrix or womb from which all things are produced. In the centre of the diagram is the Buddha Vairocana, representing the sun, or the centre of the universe, surrounded by Buddhas of the four cardinal points, with attendant Bodhisattvas. It is executed in a manner which owes more to Tibetan religious art than it does to Chinese styles. It has traditionally been described as a gift from a group of Mongol nobles to a temple under direct imperial patronage. This may have been one of the temples at the Buddhist pilgrimage site of Wutaishan, 'Mountain of the Five Terraces', in Shanxi province. Wutaishan had been a particularly holy place since at least the Tang dynasty, and was famed as the abode of the Bodhisattva Manjūsri. A popular misconception, current particularly among the Mongols who were the most devout of pilgrims, linked the name 'Manjūsri' with 'Manju', the ethnic name of the ruling house which we know as Manchu. This may partly explain the particular favour which the Qing emperors showed towards the temples of the sacred mountain.

97 (right)
BOX FOR A SPIRIT TABLET
Carved lacquer on wood
Qianlong reign period mark
(1736–95), Qing dynasty
Height 34.5 cm
FE.55-1983
Given by the Museums and Galleries
Commission from the estate of the
late Mrs L. F. Palmer
清乾隆雕漆靈牌盒

98 (overleaf)
HANGING
Mandala of the Womb Treasury World
Embroidered silk
1720–50, Qing dynasty
298 × 332 cm
FE.24-1983
Given by Sir Harry and Lady Garner
清初綉綢胎藏界曼達羅圖

Similarly inner Asian (Tibetan or Mongolian) in style is a hanging scroll or embroidered banner, worked in coloured and gilt threads in satin stitch and couching. It depicts Maitreya, the Buddha of the Future, and the focus of messianic hopes. An inscription on the back, dated to the third day of the fourth month of the forty-second year of the Qianlong reign (equivalent to 1777), is in four of the principal languages of the multi-ethnic Qing empire; Chinese, Manchu, Mongol and Tibetan. (The fifth main language, Uighur, is omitted as the Uighurs were a Muslim people.) This tells how the image was an imperial gift to an as-yet un-identified dignitary with the Tibetan name of Ngag-dbang dPal-ryor. A small numeral also on the reverse suggests that it was once part of a much larger set of religious hangings. A constant stream of gifts of this type flowed from the imperial court to temples and individuals across Asia, reinforcing the claim of the Qing emperors to be not only legitimate Sons of Heaven in Chinese terms, but also to be divinely-supported protectors of the Buddhist faith, worthy recipients of the earthly homage of all true believers.

99
HANGING SCROLL
Maitreya, Buddha of the Future
Embroidered silk
Dated 1777, Qing dynasty
76.2 × 52.1 cm
T.31-1950
清乾隆綉綢彌勒佛圖軸

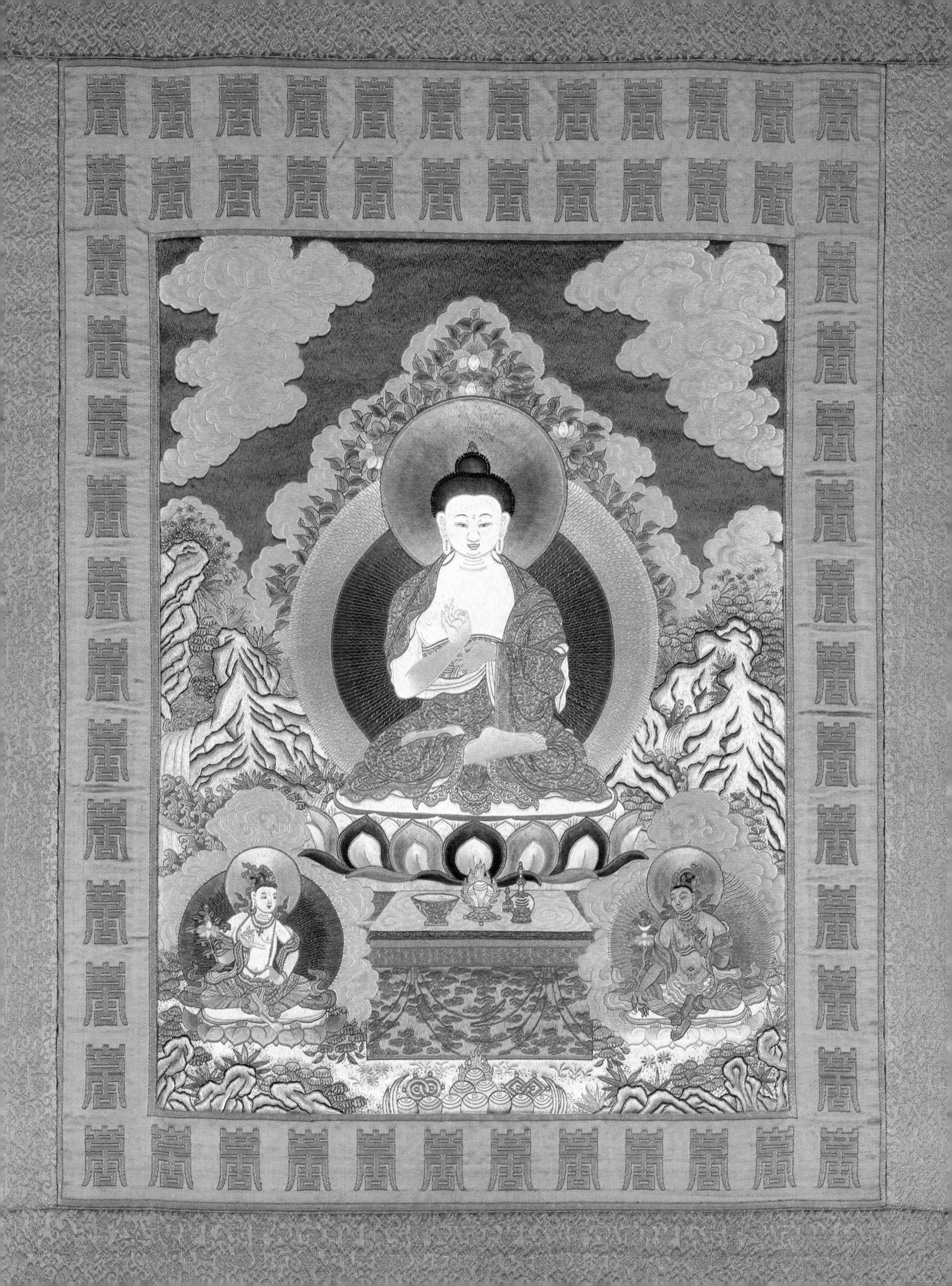

Court patronage of the arts declined from the beginning of the nineteenth century, when conscious steps were taken by two successive emperors to diminish the lavishness of their surroundings. Huge quantities of ceramics continued, however, to be ordered from Jingdezhen for occasions like imperial weddings and birthdays, and some workshops within the Forbidden City itself continued to function. One of these was the *Ruyi Guan*, 'Studio of Fulfilled Wishes', which had historically acted as a sort of design studio for a number of craft workshops, but which now produced mostly decorative paintings. Typical of its late products is the large-scale hanging scroll of highly-coloured peony blossoms (*100*), which is associated with one of the most powerful and dramatic figures of the last years of the Qing empire. This is the Dowager Empress Cixi (1835–1908) who, as mother of one emperor and aunt of another, effectively ruled China for much of the late nineteenth century. Though ruthless, reactionary and violently anti-foreign, this powerful woman, in a world where women were generally excluded from power, became in her final years a favourite of the foreign community in Peking. She ostentatiously wooed the wives of the diplomatic community, several of whom were presented with workshop paintings to which she affixed just her seal (as here), or a 'signature' with her own brush. This painting was given to Olga Julia Wegener, the wife of a relatively junior German diplomat, who served in China from 1906 to 1908.

100
HANGING SCROLL
Peonies
Ink and colours on paper
1906–08, Qing dynasty
274.5 × 82.2 cm
E.2515-1909
Wegener Gift
清末牡丹圖紙本著色軸

Collecting

THERE is a difference between the accumulation of luxury objects as signs of wealth, social prestige or political power, and the collecting of such objects as 'works of art'. Not all world cultures, whatever their aesthetic achievements, have developed the idea of the 'art work' and the 'collection'. China, however, was among the civilizations to possess this pattern of cultural activity, which gradually expanded to take in an increasing number of different types of object. The first kinds of object to be classified as 'works of art' and to be traded and collected as such, were pieces of calligraphy, inscriptions written on paper or silk with Chinese ink and brush, which were valued not for their content alone but for the aesthetic and moral force which the very forms of the characters were believed to convey. By the fourth century AD there existed the beginnings of an 'art market' in calligraphy, and the works of certain individuals were particularly treasured. It is a measure of the continued central importance of calligraphy to Chinese culture that relatively few important pieces have ever left the country. Their significance was in any case not realised by early western scholars of Chinese art, whose views informed the collections of an institution like the Victoria and Albert Museum.

This chapter looks at three periods of collecting history in China; the Song dynasty (960–1279), the Yuan and Ming dynasties (1279–1368 and 1368–1644) and the Qing dynasty (1644–1911), as well as at the way Chinese art has been collected in the western world over the last 150 years.

By the Tang dynasty (618–906) the idea of paintings as independent works of art was well established, and the first collection of artists' biographies was written, ranking painters in order of aesthetic quality, rather than by their social status. The Song dynasty saw a great expansion in the types of object to come within the system of art appreciation, in particular the bronze vessels and jade ritual objects of the early Bronze Age dynasties. These are discussed elsewhere in this book in terms of their original functions in feasting and burial rituals (pp.34, 151). They were available to Song scholars and collectors through both accidental and deliberate excavation of ancient graves and other sites. Catalogues of both state and private collections were published, some of which concentrated on any inscriptions the objects might bear, and some of which were illustrated. These latter books had a tremendous influence on the production of contemporary objects, creating a style which modern art historians have called 'archaism'. It is often not possible today to say whether an object made in the later imperial period, and imitating a Bronze Age item, was made simply in this archaistic style, or was intended to be taken for a genuine antiquity, saleable for a high price in the developed Chinese art market. Demand for art works exceeded supply, and all kinds of things were faked. Nowadays collecting has a very wide compass, and everything in the gallery, including the objects elsewhere in this book which are discussed under the heading of other

101
BRONZE COVERED VESSEL,
Dou

525–475 BC, Zhou dynasty
Height 26 cm
M.9-1935
春秋銅豆

original functions, have at some stage in their histories passed through a phase of being primarily 'collected items'. They have gone through the hands of the art market, of private collectors, and finally of institutional collectors like the Victoria and Albert Museum.

One of the achievements of Song dynasty antiquarian scholars was to tie to the forms of actual surviving or excavated objects the names for vessel shapes which are seen in very early ritual texts. These identifications have been upheld to the

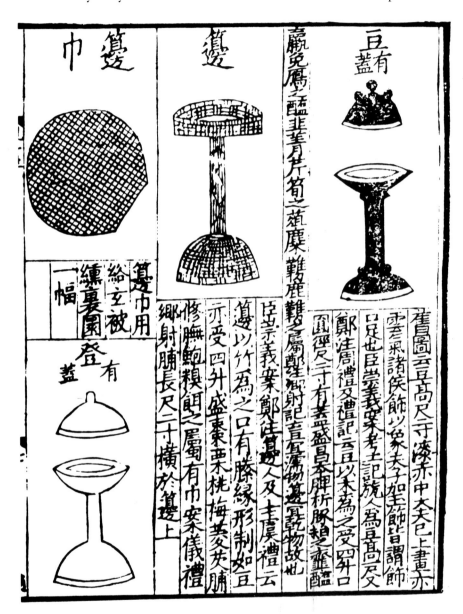

Ritual vessels, *dou* (*left*)
From < 新定三禮圖 > *Newly Ordained Illustrations for the Three Rituals* (1175)

present day. Thus the shape of the bronze standing dish and cover (*101*) was identified with the name *dou*. This example dates from about 525 to 475 BC. The degree to which these early shapes were adhered to when objects were made in later centuries can be seen from another *dou* (*102*), again of bronze but this time inlaid with gold wire in a pattern of interlaced stylized dragons and scroll ornament. The results of thermoluminescence testing of the clay core left behind within the foot by the casting process confirms a date no later than the fourteenth century AD for the base and handle, which had been joined to a much older lid.

102 (*right*)
COVERED VESSEL, *Dou*
Bronze inlaid with gold
The lid 500–400 BC, the base and handle later
Height 20.3 cm
M.978-1928
春秋錯金銅豆蓋，豆與耳後制

A group of three inlaid bronzes is shown in (*103*), the one on the left, a large jar for wine, dating to the late Zhou dynasty when this flamboyant style of decoration was at its height. It is inlaid with malachite as well as with copper. Beside it are two pieces from many centuries later, one a vessel in the shape of a goose, in the centre, and the other a kettle with a bird-headed spout, on the right. The goose displays an elaborate inlaying technique in which gold and silver wires and gold and silver sheets were inserted into pre-chiselled depressions on the surface of the bronze, slightly undercut to hold the decoration more securely. Inlaid bronzes were particularly treasured by later collectors, as it was believed throughout most of the late imperial period that they were the speciality of the Xia dynasty (traditional dates 2205–1818 BC), the most venerable of all Chinese ruling houses. Scholars today are divided about whether the Xia dynasty actually existed in the form described by the most ancient historical texts, but it is certainly the case that this period did *not* see the manufacture of bronze vessels inlaid with precious metals. The majority of the vessels believed to be of Xia date (if genuinely ancient) must have in fact come from the latter end of the Bronze Age, around the fifth to second centuries BC.

An object from the same period as the inlaid goose, which stands on the boundary between a piece destined to be used in everyday life and one intended to function purely as a collector's item, is a jade cup (*104*) dating from between 1150 and 1350. It is worked all over with a pattern of surging waves of a type also seen on the bronzes of the period, and has handles in the form of a writhing dragon and a small boy, his clothing swept by the wind as he clings precariously to the edge of the vessel. The boy is probably one of the supernatural infants who attend on the Daoist immortals, and the wind is the wind which sweeps through the upper ether which they inhabit, far above the mundane world. A short inscription on the base in an archaic form of Chinese script reads 'to be treasured forever', a form of words taken from the inscriptions seen on genuine ancient bronzes.

By the Ming dynasty, and in particular by the late sixteenth century when increased prosperity brought luxury goods and upper class cultural tastes within the reach of a wider body of consumers, the possession and display of antiques and works of art was one of the indispensable pastimes of a gentleman. The grouping of objects on a late Ming *huali* wood table (*105*) is typical of some of the most coveted and expensive pieces available through a sophisticated art market to the collectors of the day.

From right to left they are: a bronze *gui* vessel of the Zhou period, a Neolithic jade disk mounted in a Ming dynasty stand of glazed porcelain, a Ming gilt-bronze box, and a crackle-glazed stoneware vase from the Southern Song. The evidence of paintings and literature suggests such an ensemble might well have actually been used; the *gui* (though originally a food vessel) being used to burn incense contained in the bronze box, and the vase holding small tools used in its preparation. The three antique pieces would all have been extremely expensive in the late Ming dynasty, costing considerably more than contemporary painting, and more than all but the most important specimens of calligraphy from the hands of famous artists. The Ming gilt-bronze box is a more utilitarian object, though it too shows changes in the way luxury goods were treated, as it is signed by its maker with the inscription, 'made by Zhu Chenming'.

105
TABLE
Huali wood
1550–1640, Ming dynasty
Length 177 cm
FE.18-1980
明晚期花梨木案

(*left to right*)
（左至右）

VASE
Guan ware
1150–1279, Southern Song dynasty
Height 13.4 cm
C.102-1967
Barlow Gift
南宋官窯瓷瓶

BOX FOR SEAL INK
Parcel-gilt bronze
1550–1640, Ming dynasty
Diameter 9 cm
2727-1856
明晚期鍍金銅印泥盒

PORCELAIN STAND
About 1500, Ming dynasty
Height 15.3 cm
FE.4-1982
明中期瓷座

JADE DISK, *Bi*
2800–1900 BC, Neolithic
Diameter 20.3 cm
Circ.3-1933
新石器時代玉璧

BRONZE VESSEL, *Gui*
1050–950 BC, Zhou dynasty
Height 15 cm
M.1162-1926
Brooks Bequest
西周銅簋

In the late Ming period, many more makers and workshops began to add their names to their products, and these names were often discussed in texts which can be described as 'handbooks to elegant living'. These were a new type of literature which laid down rules regarding taste and elegant living, and which give an important insight into the social insecurities of an age when the traditional ruling élite worried a great deal about the *nouveaux riches* getting above themselves. Books of this type, such as *Eight Discourses on the Art of Living* (1591) and the *Treatise on Superfluous Things* by Wen Zhenheng (1585–1645), contain extremely detailed prescriptions on which objects are 'elegant' and which are 'vulgar'. For example, the table shown (*105*) would have displeased Wen Zhenheng, since the panels

Two gentlemen in a garden (*below*)
Illustration to the drama
< 櫻桃夢 > *A Dream of Cherries*
(1573–1619)

between its legs are carved in openwork with a design of writhing dragons emerging from and turning into luxuriant vegetation, a decorative motif which he denounced as 'vulgar' if used on this particular shape of table.

The literature of Ming connoisseurs is full of anxieties about and warnings against buying fakes. Forgery of very valuable ancient pieces was rife in the bronze-making and jade-working crafts, as well as in the fields of painting, calligraphy and ceramics. Anything which could be collected could be faked, and great attention was paid by forgers of bronzes to reproducing the surface patination caused on a genuine piece by centuries of burial. As well as the manufacture of totally fraudulent pieces, parts of genuine objects were combined with modern components to form showy composite vessels, as Gao Lian, author of *Eight Discourses on the Art of Living*, recorded. The inlaid vase shown on the left of (*106*) was made from at least

106 (*opposite*)
VASE (*left*)
Bronze inlaid with gold and silver
The tubes 206 BC–AD 8, with later mountings
Height 20 cm
M.730-1910
Salting Bequest
西漢錯金銀銅雙聯瓶，後加配飾

JADE JAR WITH LID (*right*)
1550–1640, Ming dynasty
Height 10.8 cm
FE.47-1980
明晚期帶蓋玉卮

seven pieces, analysis revealing that the metal of the two central tubes is totally different in composition to that of the supporting structure. These tubes are inlaid in sheet gold and silver with patterns of spirals and flames, as well as tiny animals and humans with animal heads, all executed in the style of the Han dynasty. The tubes are thus likely to have been originally some sort of fitting, possibly part of a chariot, made in the second century BC. Many centuries later, probably somewhere between 1100 and 1500, they were mounted on a base, to which were attached the figures of a supporting feline beast and a fabulous bird, before the whole thing was encrusted with red and green patination.

The jade lidded jar illustrated on the right with the vase shows the complexity of the situation with regard to the faking of antiquities in the late Ming period. It is in the style of jade cups from the late Bronze Age, imitating the form and decoration closely. At least one very similar vessel has been excavated in China bearing the signature of Lu Zigang (active about 1560–1600), renowned in his own time and subsequently as the greatest of jade workers. This signed piece cannot have been intended to pass as an antiquity, and so it would be unwise to call the illustrated jar a 'fake'. It is not the intrinsic qualities of form or decoration which make an object either a 'fake' or an honest reinterpretation of ancient styles, but rather the social context in which it was used, something which we cannot now recapture. Perhaps the same jade cup has been used in both ways in the centuries since it was made.

It was in the Ming period that the collecting of ceramics as works of art assumed the importance which it has held down to the present day. Ming collectors first defined the various 'wares' into which Chinese stoneware and porcelain have been divided for convenience. These are mostly geographical names, related to the centres of production of the various types. Thus the tall vase shown in the centre of the display cabinet (107), made in the Song or Yuan periods in the shape of an ancient jade cong, would be defined as 'Longquan ware', after the region of Zhejiang province where the kilns were situated. To the left of it is a vessel in the shape of an incense burner, of a type which has long been a puzzle to collectors. The connoisseurship literature of the Ming period reveals that the most valued of all ceramic types, the centrepiece of any collection, was considered to be an incense burner of 'Ding ware', a white porcelain manufactured in the Song period in north China. The Ding kilns seem to have manufactured almost no vessels in the incense burner shape, and so it seems likely that this piece is one of a group of objects manufactured much later at the major porcelain producing centre of Jingdezhen to fill the gap in the market.

The enamelled porcelain cup shown nearby is, by contrast, a piece of the highest quality manufactured to court order in the Chenghua reign of the Ming dynasty (1465–87). By the late sixteenth century, the porcelains manufactured under the early Ming rulers had changed their status from being just luxurious but practical items, to being art objects sought by collectors. Few types were more desired than the Chenghua 'chicken cups', delicately painted in the technique known as 'dovetailing colours', where blue painted under the glaze and enamels added over it fit harmoniously together. As was standard in China, the cup is shown on a small wooden stand. These stands were an integral part of the display of three-dimensional art works of all types in the Ming and Qing dynasties, and have remained popular with Chinese collectors to the present. Unfortunately, they were thought

107
DISPLAY CABINET
Huali wood
1600–1700, Ming-Qing dynasties
Height 122.5 cm
FE.14-1980
明末 — 清初花梨木櫃

(*shown inside it, left to right*)
(櫃內展物左至右)

PORCELAIN INCENSE
BURNER
1550–1640, Ming dynasty
Height 11.1 cm
Circ.130-1935
明晚期瓷簋爐

VASE IN FORM OF A JADE
Cong
Porcelain with green glaze
1250–1350, Song-Yuan dynasties
Height 27 cm
Circ.125-1938
南宋 — 元瓷琮瓶

WINE CUP
Porcelain painted in enamels
Chenghua reign period mark
(1465–87), Ming dynasty
Diameter 8.3 cm
C.1-1960
明成化釉上彩瓷酒杯

INCENSE BURNER
Bronze inlaid with gold and silver
1550–1640, Ming dynasty
Height 10.4 cm
FE.43-1980
明晚期錯金銀銅鼎爐

by early western collectors and curators of Chinese art to detract from the object, and many original stands have been discarded.

The display cabinet itself is one of a pair and is divided into an upper section where a number of objects might be shown, and a lower section where the majority of the pieces in a collection would have been stored in fitted boxes until the opportunity arose to bring them out for discussion and enjoyment with fellow connoisseurs.

Paintings generally were stored in this way. None of the main Chinese formats for paintings were meant to be placed on permanent display like the western oil on canvas; small pictures were mounted in albums while larger works took the form of horizontal hand scrolls or vertical hanging scrolls, both of which were brought out as the season, the occasion and the owner's mood dictated. The technical resources necessary to produce a painting on silk or paper were largely the same as those used for writing, and thus were within the reach of all literate people, unlike the special technologies of bronze casting or jade working. This meant that there were few barriers in the way of the production of large quantities of fraudulent antique paintings.

Just what such an item could look like in the late Ming period is suggested by a large scale hanging scroll (*108*) showing a gentleman accompanied by his servant approaching a cottage in the mountains to pay a visit on a friend. The work is signed at the bottom right hand corner by Li Zhaodao (active about 670–730) and carries the seals and inscriptions of a number of famous connoisseurs, including Ke Jiusi (1290–1343) and Wen Zhengming (1470–1559). In purely stylistic terms the attribution is preposterous. The painting makes no attempt to imitate what was thought at the time to be a Tang dynasty style, nor even to conform to the type of landscape style, lavishly worked with blue and green mineral pigments, which was particularly associated in the art historical literature with Li Zhaodao (none of whose works in fact survive). Ming purchasers, however, particularly those insecure about their own artistic discernment, were likely to pay far more attention to the authenticating inscriptions and seals than they would to the actual features of the brushwork, and it is on these that the forger has lavished most care and attention.

108
HANGING SCROLL
Visiting a Friend in the Mountains
Ink and colours on paper
1550–1600, Ming dynasty
177.8 × 96.5 cm
E.422-1953
Sharples Bequest
明晚期 < 攜琴訪友圖 >
紙本墨彩軸

One probably genuine work from the Museum's very small collection of Chinese painting is a hanging scroll (*109*) by Xiang Shengmo (1597–1658). It shows a bunch of camellias bound together with grasses and is painted in ink alone, on a ground of absorbent paper. It is signed on the right, above one of the eighty or more seals which Xiang used at various stages of his career. At the bottom left of the picture is the seal of a later collector, reading 'painting treasured in the collection of Mr Gao'. The artist is closely linked to one of the greatest art collections of the late Ming period, that of his grandfather Xiang Yuanbian (1525–90). Xiang Yuanbian had come from a merchant background, rather than from the class of officials and landowners who dominated Chinese politics and society, but he was acceptable to the ruling élite largely because of his unparalleled collection of masterpieces of painting and calligraphy. In later centuries, many objects claiming to have been owned by him were fraudulently manufactured, and his collection seals were added to a large number of paintings which were either fake or, though genuine, never actually owned by him.

The technology of woodblock printing, first used in China in the ninth century, played an important part in spreading awareness of artistic matters among the Chinese élite. Illustrated catalogues of antiquities were produced from the eleventh century, and collections of reproductions of famous paintings from the sixteenth century. At the very beginning of the seventeenth century Chinese printers mastered the technique of producing colour prints from a number of separate wooden blocks, enabling them to imitate closely the effects of painted brushwork. This was used to great effect in a work entitled the *Mustard Seed Garden Manual of Painting* (*110*), the first part of which was published in Nanjing in 1679, with parts two and three appearing in 1701. The page shown comes from Part Three, which is mostly a didactic manual of brushwork techniques, and is one of the full-colour illustrations designed by the painter, Wang Gai (active about 1679–1705). They may have been intended as models for emulation and guides to the laying on of colour, or more possibly simply to provide pleasure in their own right.

109
HANGING SCROLL
Bunch of Flowers
By Xiang Shengmo (1597–1658)
62.9 × 33.6 cm
FE.5-1974
Given by Sir Harry and Lady Garner
明項聖謨繪 ＜ 花草圖 ＞ 軸

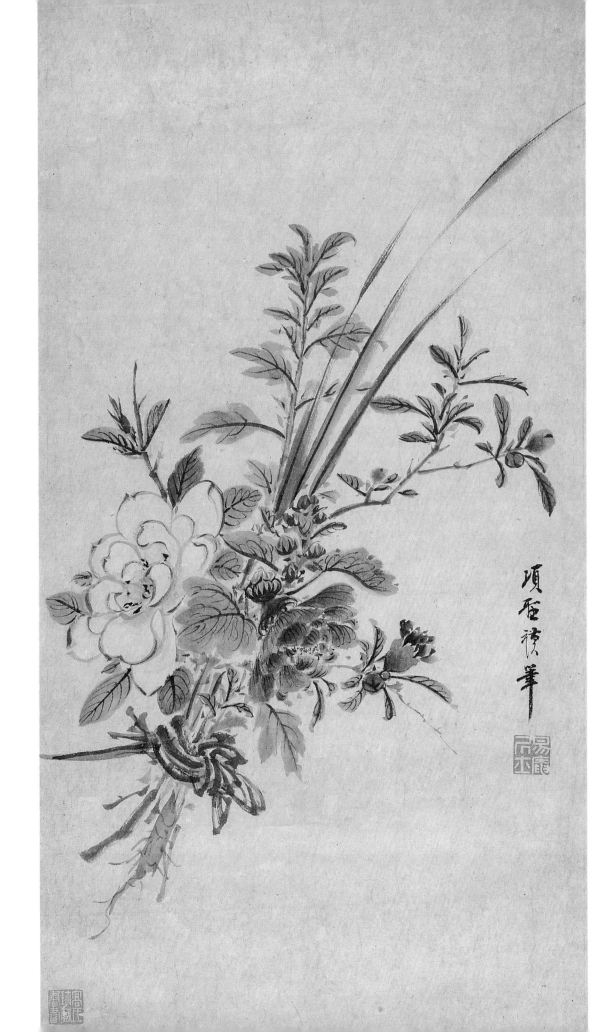

若欲滿盤
堆馬乳莫
辭添尒引
龍鬚

110
COLOUR PRINT FROM
WOODBLOCKS
From *The Mustard Seed Garden Manual
of Painting*, Part III
Designed by Wang Gai (active about
1679–1705)
1701, Qing dynasty
30.5 × 37.3 cm
E.4779-1916
Alexander Gift
清康熙王概編 ＜芥子園畫譜＞
木版彩印圖

The collectors of the Qing dynasty continued all the interests of their Ming predecessors in terms of calligraphy, painting, antiquities and early ceramics, but they also added an interest in contemporary miniature crafts like carving and snuff bottles (57). Indeed it seems likely that some of these bottles (see p.136) were produced for a market of collectors, and were never actually used. Shown on a wooden stand of early twentieth century date, on the right of plate (111), is a small vase of early Qing date, naturalistically carved to represent the stump of a pine tree. The unidentified hardstone has been stained artificially, and the flat base bears the name 'Shangjun', an alternative name used by the carver Zhou Bin, together with a cyclical date. Zhou Bin is variously recorded in later sources as active throughout most of the seventeenth century, so the date could be equivalent to either 1641 or 1701. The fame of this artist, who specialized in carving the soft soapstone found in the south-western coastal provinces of Zhejiang and Fujian, was such that many pieces have been attributed to him, either at their time of manufacture, or by adding his name subsequently.

On the left of the stand is an elaborate and highly decorated cup of rhinoceros horn, the body of which is covered with the writhing mythical beast called *chi hu* in Chinese. The decorative scheme is very loosely derived from the bronze vessels of ancient times, though the shape of the vessel is a fantasy of the carver, rather than a precise imitation of an earlier form. By the time it was made, it was probably intended purely as a display piece rather than, like (67), a vessel intended to add medicinal elements to the food contained within it.

111

RHINOCEROS HORN CUP
(*left*)
1600–1700, Ming-Qing dynasties
Height 15.8 cm
162-1879
明末 — 清初雕犀牛角杯

CARVED HARDSTONE VASE
By Zhou Bin (active 17th century)
1641 or 1701, Ming or Qing dynasty
Height 10.2 cm
5526-1901
明末 — 清初周彬雕石瓶

DISPLAY STAND
Hardwood and burl wood
1920–25, Republic
Length 41.9 cm
W.15-1925
現代硬木樹疤几

The whole field of antiquarianism and collecting in the Qing period was affected by the fact that the greatest and most energetic collectors, at least in the eighteenth century, were the emperors themselves (see pp.198–208). The precision of Qing antiquarianism, and its dependence on court taste, were fed by the production of catalogues of the imperial collections, which were illustrated by woodblock printing (see p.232). An eighteenth-century lacquered wooden cup in the form known as a *jue* on the right of (*112*) clearly depends quite closely (allowing for the different demands of casting in metal and carving in lacquer) on its Bronze Age prototype, on the right of the picture. The lacquer artist would have been able to draw for the shape on the four precisely delineated examples in the *Imperially Ordained Mirror of Antiquities Prepared in the Xiqing Hall*, of 1749. By the Qing period, a more detached and scholarly view of how to treat the surviving objects of the distant past prevailed. Back in 1486, when the scholar painter, Shen Zhou (1427–1509) celebrated what was by Chinese reckoning his sixtieth birthday, at the party in his honour he fastened his robe with an ancient jade buckle, and drank wine from a Shang dynasty bronze *jue*, presumably like the example shown. This behaviour, with its air of a deep communion with the most remote phases of Chinese culture, was not unusual in the Ming period, but by the eighteenth century it would have seemed rather more strange, even outlandish. To the scholars of the Qianlong reign and after, a *jue* was the object of a reinvigorated classical scholarship, which made great advances in the study of ancient inscriptions, and laid the foundations for the academic study of Chinese art history and archaeology in our own time.

112
POURING VESSEL, *Jue* (*left*)
Bronze
1100–1000 BC, Shang-Zhou dynasties
Height 21 cm
M.3-1950
商末— 西周初銅爵

POURING VESSEL, *Jue*
(*right*)
Carved lacquer on wood
1750–1800, Qing dynasty
Height 17.6 cm
FE.62-1974
Given by Sir Harry and Lady Garner
清中期雕漆爵

Chinese ceramics had been highly regarded in Europe from the middle ages, and by the seventeenth century a flourishing export trade was established, shipping millions of pieces a year to the West as an adjunct to the more important trade in tea and silk. Such export items were, however, largely made especially for foreign tastes. It was only in the middle of the nineteenth century that collectors and scholars, first in France and then in Britain, began trying to understand those aspects of Chinese art which related to the domestic market. They affected to despise things made specifically for the export trade, but their concentration on certain materials (above all on ceramics), and their complete ignorance of other art forms (such as calligraphy) meant that their view of 'Chinese art' remained one seen through a heavily distorted filter. This primacy given to ceramics was the view adopted by the South Kensington Museum (forerunner of the V&A), which from its inception in the middle of the nineteenth century eagerly collected those types of Chinese object which had found a place in western taste.

The largest single category at this period was certainly that of Qing dynasty ceramics, divided into wares decorated in underglaze blue and those enamelled over the glaze. This latter type was further subdivided in 1862 by the French writer Jacquemart into the three 'families': *famille verte*, *famille rose* and *famille noire*, depending on the colour of the background enamel. *Famille noire* (*113*) was the object of an extraordinary outburst of enthusiasm on the part of western collectors, well out of proportion to its status in China. Very high prices were paid for black glazed vases, many of them being frauds produced to meet the excessive demand, until tastes changed and these lavishly decorated porcelains declined in estimation.

113
VASE
Porcelain decorated in enamels
Kangxi reign period (1662–1722),
Qing dynasty
Height 46 cm
C.1304-1910
Salting Bequest
清康熙珐瑯彩瓷瓶

As far as the early period of collecting at the V&A is concerned, the key figure was undoubtedly George Salting (1835–1909) who bequeathed to the Museum, along with huge collections of European art, a very large number of Qing porcelains. The lidded 'hawthorn ginger jar' from his collection (*114*) is one of a group of three which fetched the then considerable sum of £830 in 1887, when the aesthetic movement and the accompanying craze for blue and white porcelain were at their peak. The term 'ginger jar' is purely conventional, as there is no evidence that these pieces were intended for this purpose when manufactured in the late seventeenth or early eighteenth century. Their decoration of early prunus blossoms against a background of cracked ice may simply signify that they were intended as presents appropriate to the New Year.

In the early part of this century the interest of collectors of Chinese art in Britain continued to centre on ceramics (European and American collectors in many cases had different tastes). Many advances in the study of the subject were made not by

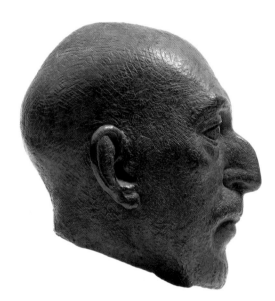

George Eumorfopoulos (*left*)
Bronze head by Dora Gordine FRBS
A.12-1944

114 (*right*)
JAR
Porcelain decorated in underglaze blue
Kangxi reign period (1662–1722),
Qing dynasty
Height 23 cm
C.819-1910
Salting Bequest
清康熙青花瓷罐

institutions but by private collectors, several of whom owned collections surpassing those of the national institutions. In 1921 the Oriental Ceramic Society was formed in London, with an initial membership of twelve men who aimed 'to widen appreciation and to acquire knowledge of Eastern Ceramic Art.' Perhaps the best-known and most influential collector of this inter-war period was George Eumorfopoulos (1862–1939), whose huge collection was divided between the British Museum and the V&A. The four objects shown (*115*) were all acquired by the Museum in the decade between 1926 and 1936, the period in which a new canon of taste, symbolised by the Eumorfopoulos Collection, was established.

This no longer favoured the enamelled and highly decorated porcelain of the late imperial period, which had been prized by an earlier generation of collectors. The taste now was for the less obviously 'finished' wares of the Song period, which were felt to embody ideals of 'vitality'; ideals which were derived ultimately from the philosopher Henri Bergson and from Carl Jung. One of the most influential figures in promoting this new approach to Chinese ceramics was the potter Bernard Leach (1887–1979), much of whose own work was inspired by Song dynasty forms and decoration.

115 (left to right)

VASE

Painted Cizhou ware
1115–1200, Jin dynasty
Height 24.1 cm
C.32-1935
金磁州窰繪釉瓷瓶

VASE

1115–1200, Jin dynasty
Height 47.6 cm
C.812-1936
金褐釉瓷瓶

BOWL

Ding ware
1050–1150, Song-Jin dynasties
Diameter 28.5 cm
C.217-1926
宋 — 金定窰瓷碗

BOWL

Longquan ware with 'duck's egg blue'
glaze and gold rim
1150–1279, Southern Song dynasty
Diameter 12.7 cm
C.26-1935
南宋龍泉窰金口卵青釉瓷碗

In the post-war decades, western collectors' taste in Chinese ceramics shifted once again, with the highest esteem being reserved for Yuan and early Ming blue and white porcelain (*116*). The bowl illustrated came in to the Museum in 1951, at a time when many of the big pre-war collections were being dispersed. It has many of the characteristics that would have pleased a Chinese collector, being in good condition, and of demonstrable 'imperial quality'. This phrase is used to denote pieces which by their form and style of decoration, and above all from the fact that they have an imperial reign mark written on them, can be identified as having been made at the imperial porcelain factory for court use. English sales catalogues of the early 1950s, however, made much of proven 'English' provenances of such items. The incidence of objects being shown at exhibitions in Great Britain was always recorded, and on occasion auctioneers found such phrases as the following useful to sales:

> We are informed that every item in this Collection was acquired in England before December, 1950.

The previous emphasis on ceramics began to give way to a certain extent to a wider view of Chinese art, though with the People's Republic itself being inaccessible until quite recently it was still a view conditioned by the holdings of western museums. In Britain these state institutions largely took over from the great private collectors as the principal promoters of the study of Chinese art history, although private patrons continue to build up significant collections in America and the Far East. The individual tastes and personal insights of collectors like Mr T. T. Tsui continue to provide a counterpart to the academic study in universities and museums of China's past achievements.

116
BOWL
Porcelain decorated in underglaze blue
Xuande reign period mark (1426–35),
Ming dynasty
Diameter 27 cm
C.310-1951
明宣德青花瓷缸

The Victoria and Albert Museum was originally intended to be a source for the collection and study of contemporary design in the widest international sense. With regard to Chinese design, this intention was for most of the twentieth century superseded simply by collecting artefacts from the historic past; it has now been reaffirmed. In recent years the holdings of Chinese material have been enlarged with the products of the period since the establishment of the People's Republic of China in 1949.

The V&A now houses one of the largest collections of modern Chinese craft and design outside China itself. The tall lacquer vase on the right of (*117*), dating from 1951, is in the 'bodiless' lacquer technique particularly associated with Fujian province. Its full-blown romantic decoration of a dazzling red sunrise is typical of the imagery favoured at the dawn of the Chinese Communist Party's power, yet the object was produced in a factory which was still privately owned, before the collectivisation of craft production which occurred later in the 1950s.

The vase is shown with a glazed pottery pickle jar, on the left, made at Rongchang in Sichuan province in 1965. This demonstrates another abiding theme in modern Chinese design, the search for an 'authentic' decorative language, to be derived from the folk-life of the 'masses', rather than the tastes of the imperial court or the scholar bureaucrats. These Sichuan ceramics were one of the more successful attempts to graft popular traditions onto the sort of art education now provided by China's numerous art colleges.

117
VASE (*right*)
Painted lacquer on fabric
1951
Height 46 cm
FE.36-1989
現代彩繪脫胎漆瓶

PICKLE JAR (*left*)
Glazed stoneware
1965
Height 24 cm
FE.38-1989
現代釉瓷罐

A key figure in the attempt was the principal of the Sichuan School of Art, the lacquer artist, theoretician and art educator, Shen Fuwen (born 1906). He had trained as a painter and woodcut artist before studying lacquering in Japan under one of that country's greatest modern craftsmen, Matsuda Gonroku (1896–1986). The Museum owns a number of works by Shen, the most recent being a plate on the left of (*118*) made in 1985. The style could perhaps be loosely described as 'Tang revival', with a central motif of a duck with foliage in its beak surrounded by stylized petals and dots of mother of pearl. The Dunhuang caves of the Tang period (see p.88) have been an abiding source of artistic inspiration in China since the 1940s, as the principal alternative to more conservative styles derived from the art of the eighteenth century. The grip which Dunhuang has retained on the Chinese artistic imagination is suggested by a comparison of the Shen Fuwen plate with a porcelain plate, on the right, decorated in 'Tang' style in underglaze blue and designed over thirty years previously by the painter, Zhu Danian (born 1915). It formed part of a commission to design tableware for the showcase Peking Hotel, reopened in 1952, and was one of the key attempts to create a 'national' design idiom for the People's Republic, free of some of the connotations of the more recent imperial past.

118

PLATE (*left*)

Painted lacquer on wood, inlaid with mother of pearl
By Shen Fuwen (born 1906)
1985
Diameter 35 cm
FE.26-1989
現代沈福文造嵌螺漆繪盤

PLATE (*right*)

Porcelain decorated in underglaze blue
Designed by Zhu Danian (born 1915)
1952
Diameter 23 cm
FE.40-1989
現代祝大年設計青花瓷碟

Index

Figures in [*brackets*] refer to illustration numbers.